KV-014-033

Cosmopolitan
Criticism

MA
5827.
A3 B7

❧ Cosmopolitan Criticism

Oscar Wilde's Philosophy of Art

Julia Prewitt Brown

University Press of Virginia
Charlottesville and London

The University Press of Virginia
© 1997 by the Rector and Visitors of the University of Virginia
All rights reserved
Printed in the United States of America

First published 1997

∞ The paper in this publication meets the minimum requrements of the
American National Standard for Information Sciences—Permanence of Paper for
Printed Library Materials, ANSI Z39.48-1984.

Library of Congress Cataloging-in-Publication Data

Brown, Julia Prewitt, 1948–
    Cosmopolitan criticism : Oscar Wilde's philosophy of art / Julia
Prewitt Brown.
      p.   cm.
    Includes bibliographical references (p.   ) and index.
    ISBN 0-8139-1728-X (cloth : alk. paper)
    1. Wilde, Oscar, 1854–1900—Aesthetics.   2. Art and literature—
Great Britain—History—19th century.   3. Wilde, Oscar, 1854–1900—
Influence.   4. Aesthetics, British—19th century.   5. Aesthetic
movement (British art)   6. Aestheticism (Literature)   7. Aesthetics,
Modern.   I. Title.
PR5827.A35B76   1997
828'.809—dc21   96-37986
                                                                  CIP

314390

The Critical Spirit and the World-Spirit are one.
　　　　　　　　　　　　　　　　　　—Oscar Wilde, 1891

❧ Contents

℘ Acknowledgments

AMONG THOSE who at various points have helped me with this book are Christopher Ricks, John Paul Riquelme, Norma Kroll, Leland Monk, and Michael Prince; to them I am especially grateful. A grant from the Mellon Foundation enabled me to study at Harvard University for a year during the early stages of research. I wish to thank as well members of the Humanities Foundation seminar of 1991–92 at Boston University, especially Katherine T. O'Connor, for the opportunity to present part of the manuscript and receive valuable suggestions. Dahlia Rudavsky supported this work during its difficult stages; I thank her for her perseverance and dedication to principle. And without the conversation of Carol McGuirk, writing the book would have been far less interesting and enjoyable.

Most of all, I wish to thank my husband, Howard Eiland, for his patient editing of the manuscript and for giving me the benefit of his learning.

❧ A Note on Texts and Abbreviations

UNLESS OTHERWISE indicated, all references to Wilde's works are from *The First Collected Edition of Oscar Wilde's Works*, edited by Robert Ross. For convenience, I have used the following abbreviations to refer to works cited frequently in the body of the text. Full bibliographic information can be found in the Select Bibliography.

DG   *The Picture of Dorian Gray*
DP   *De Profundis* or "To Lord Alfred Douglas." *Selected Letters of Oscar Wilde*. Ed. Rupert Hart-Davis. 152–240
I   *Intentions and The Soul of Man*
M   *Miscellanies*
ON   *Oscar Wilde's Oxford Notebooks*. Ed. Philip E. Smith and Michael S. Helfand
R   *Reviews*

Nietzsche's works are abbreviated as follows:

A   *The Antichrist*
BG   *Beyond Good and Evil*
EH   *Ecce Homo*
GM   *On the Genealogy of Morals*
JW   *Joyful Wisdom*
TI   *Twilight of the Idols*
WP   *The Will to Power*
Z   *Thus Spoke Zarathustra*

𝕾 Preface

THIS BOOK is about what I believe to be Oscar Wilde's most important, but also—especially today when it is in danger of being lost sight of altogether—most elusive legacy, his philosophy of art: of what art is and is not, of what the experience of art means in the modern world, and of the contradictory relations of the work of art to the sphere of "life," to the ethical, the pragmatic, the everyday. Since Wilde's ideas on these subjects developed over time, I underscore the evolving, experimental character of his thought, taking *De Profundis* to represent the culmination of the Wildean aesthetic speculations. In this widely misunderstood and underestimated work the life of the artist, in all its inspired excess, enters most intimately into the subject and form of his art.

Virtually everything Wilde wrote after 1888 bears the stamp of his long-standing preoccupation with a certain philosophic problematic—we may label it postdualist—that was in many respects definitive for the late nineteenth century. In fact the resemblance of his critical and philosophical writing to that of his contemporary, Friedrich Nietzsche, was quickly noted.[1] Like that of Nietzsche or of Schiller, Novalis, and Baudelaire before him, Wilde's aesthetic theory was closely tied to a political vision, however unsystematic. In his case, he recognized both the ethical advantages of socialism—he believed it would make possible a fuller flowering of individualism than could ever be engendered under the aegis of private property—*and* the aesthetic limitations of the socialist vision, its tendency to bypass the question of art. It was characteristic of Wilde the philosopher to seek a solution that would satisfy both ethical and aesthetic imperatives. Convinced that the future of art, as well as of civilization as a whole, depended on the development of what he called "cosmopolitan criticism," Wilde consciously made himself at home in the culture of other nations. This internal and external emigration, however, did not entail a repudiation of his own roots, any more than the cosmopolitanism of James Joyce or of Henry James signified a denial of the importance of national character. Wilde's cosmopolitanism was therefore dialectical in nature, in a sense which Wilde, as a reader of Hegel, would most likely appreciate, even though he himself did not take up this term.

In the chapters to follow, we shall see that Wilde made a distinctly Anglo-Irish contribution to an international tradition of ideas on art, a contribution composed of several different but interrelated elements: the theory of cosmopolitan criticism, the inquiry into the diminishing and equivocal place of art in the postindustrial world, and the great improvisation of his own life. Before we delve into these subjects, however, a brief overview of some of the main currents of the criticism on Wilde will clarify the terms and objectives of *Cosmopolitan Criticism*.

In 1971 Lionel Trilling noted that Wilde's importance as a thinker was steadily growing, and he predicted that such intellectual consequence would soon cease to be overshadowed by the spectacle of his "posturing" and "martyrdom."[2] Other notable evaluations of Wilde had already appeared: Edouard Roditi's study of 1947, which drew attention to modern literature's debt to Wilde, Alick West's illuminating (and now rarely cited) essay on Pater and Wilde in *The Mountain in the Sunlight* (1958), and Richard Ellmann's Introduction to *The Artist as Critic* in 1968 are three examples.[3] Despite the proliferation of articles and books on Wilde in the decades following Trilling's assessment, however, his prediction has not on the whole been borne out. The attention of Anglo-American critics to the material conditions for the production of works of art—and the prevailing notion of culture as ideology—has led to a new emphasis on Wilde as a professional writer, together with a general neglect of his philosophy of criticism and art.[4] The "martyrdom" that in Trilling's view precluded a proper grasp of Wilde's achievement has now become the basis for theories of homosexual identity;[5] the "posturing" is seen as an essential element in Wilde's formation of an audience, a kind of self-commodification that links Wilde's career to the emergence of a consumerist economy and culture.[6] In short, the high esteem in which Wilde was held as a thinker by W. K. Wimsatt and Lionel Trilling, and more recently by Harold Bloom, has not led to the appreciation of Wilde's critical writing that one might have expected. Although there are important exceptions,[7] current trends in "materialist" criticism are not often attuned to the manifestly idealist bent of Wilde's thought; it would seem that his spiritual pleasures offend contemporary pieties scarcely less than his bodily pleasures offended the Victorians. This is all the more unfortunate when one considers that it is the great cosmopolitan-materialist critics, such as Theodor Adorno and Walter Benjamin (critics whom Wilde in some ways prefigures), who were most alive to the very questions Wilde poses concerning the nature of art.

The major challenge to the contemporary trends in Wilde criticism already noted may be said to have come from Wilde himself, in the form of the 1989 publication of the notebooks that he kept at Oxford in the late 1870s. Scrupulously edited and introduced by Philip E. Smith and Michael S. Helfand, the *Oxford Notebooks* show the extent to which Wilde drew on readings in philosophy, history, and science to develop the philosophical taxonomy by which he would later come to treat the problem of art. The editors' argument, advanced in two introductory essays, is that Wilde achieved a synthesis of philosophical idealism and evolutionary theory while he was at Oxford, and that this synthesis is reenacted throughout Wilde's critical essays, dialogues, and novel. Although I take exception to the word *synthesis*—my own argument is that throughout his career Wilde maintained a paradoxical interrelatedness of opposites that was no mere synthesis—I am indebted to Smith and Helfand for illuminating the original philosophical orientation and context of Wilde's thought. In the *Notebooks*, Wilde drew on pure metaphysics and pure science so as to understand their limitations in relation to one another. Only in art, wherein spirit is embodied in the sensuous, do the ideal and empirical realms realize themselves and become "true."

To turn our attention to Wilde's philosophy of art, therefore, is not to revert to a narrow or naive idealism. As is shown here, the aestheticism developed in Wilde's writing cannot be reduced to a simple assertion of the predominance of beauty or the autonomy and disinterestedness of art—the conventional position of the fin-de-siècle aesthete. Although Wilde adopted this position in a witty, self-advertising manner early in his career, it is clear that even then his animadversions against "morality" refer to the puritan and philistine moralities of the period. Wilde asserted the centrality of the aesthetic imagination, but not as something divorced from moral and spiritual life. His claim that aesthetics is "higher" than ethics, as the context in which it is uttered makes clear, is based on definitions of both terms that understand the aesthetic to transform, rather than transcend, the ethical. Thus the serious work of art can never be directly "moral" in its effects, as many of Wilde's contemporaries wished it to be; it could never bolster conventional ways of thinking, although it could spiritualize the individual and, unlike a self-deceiving philanthropy, help to develop the "simple and spontaneous virtue that there is in man" (*I* 188–89). Most important: by intellectual or cosmopolitan criticism, Wilde meant a form of aesthetic experience that, in engaging the art of other cultures together with that of one's own, had the power to accomplish what neither abstract systems of ethics nor humanitarian sympathy could achieve: to make other nations a part of one's native heritage. "One had ancestors in literature," we are told, "as well as in one's own race" (*DG* 232).

I argue that Wilde's calculated dodginess, his outward strivings to elude definition, had a profound philosophical significance. For he was always aiming to overcome, and ultimately for a moment did overcome, in both his life and his writing, the separation of morality and aesthetics that governed the thought of so many nineteenth-century writers, and that in the course of the century was more and more experienced as an opposition. Two examples will serve: the separation of the ethically ordering principle of "mechanism" from the aesthetic and spiritual principle of the "dynamic" in Carlyle's thought, and the division between Hellenism, or spontaneity of consciousness, and Hebraism, strictness of conscience, in Arnold's *Culture and Anarchy*. Although Carlyle acknowledges that the mechanical and the dynamic represent different human capacities, he sets them off against one another in "Signs of the Times," and although Arnold's Hellenism and Hebraism may represent the two fundamental, intertwined traditions of our civilization (namely, the classical and the biblical), he opposes them in his discussion of the battle between culture and anarchy in modern England. Wilde's cosmopolitanism—which must be distinguished from internationalism on the one hand and eclecticism on the other— figures centrally in the overcoming of these oppositions.[8] Through the transforming critical spirit of cosmopolitanism, propounded earlier in the century by Baudelaire, Wilde came to terms with the immense contradictions within the Victorian prose writers, both as individuals and as a group: the contradiction within *Culture and Anarchy*, for example, between its nationalism and its call for disinterestedness, or the contradiction between Arnold's integral and Mill's aggregate conceptions of the state.

It will be remarked that Walter Pater's place in the particular intellectual history already alluded to here is relatively minor, and that far less is said in the following pages about Pater's influence on Wilde than about Wilde's divergence from Pater. With attention to the philosophical significance of Wilde's career, this loosening of the long-established tie between Pater and Wilde constitutes the main revisionary thrust of this book. The two revaluations of Wilde are in fact related, for not least among Wilde's achievements is his transcendence of Pater's impressionism. In the famous conclusion to *The Renaissance*, Pater founds all knowledge on the bundle of sensations. Art may offer us sense experiences of a quality higher than those of other sensations, but the experiences are not of an essentially different quality. Subordinating his aestheticism to a science of "physical life," the atomism of "natural elements to which science gives their names,"[9] Pater remains securely tied to the tradition of English empiricism deriving from Locke and Hume.

Wilde transcends Pater's subjectivism not by denying it but by assimilating and going beyond it in the manner of Kant. Exposed to Kant's critical idealism as early as his days at Trinity College, Dublin, Wilde concludes in his Oxford Commonplace Book that "Kant showed the insufficiency of the empiricism of Hume" by pointing out the "universal and necessary character" of subjective categories of thought (*ON* 128). Questioning the one-sided presuppositions of materialism throughout his career, Wilde was always a larger and more supple thinker than Pater partly because he was always intent on developing within his imagination the various continental influences to which his most important predecessors— Carlyle, Coleridge and, above all, Arnold—had opened the door. When Wilde published *Intentions* in 1891, so striking was his departure from the solipsistic aestheticism of Pater that Pater himself designated Wilde as Arnold's true successor, praising the author for carrying on, "more perhaps than any other writer, the brilliant critical work of Matthew Arnold."[10]

In the act of transforming Victorian social and aesthetic criticism, then, Wilde takes his place in a European tradition of thought that stretches from Kant and Schiller, through Kierkegaard and Nietzsche, to the preeminent cosmopolitan artist-critics of this century, Benjamin and Adorno. The cosmopolitan criticism that Wilde inherited from authors as diverse as Baudelaire, Ruskin, and Arnold receives its fulfillment, we might say, in Benjamin's work; and it may be in the context of Benjamin's bold thinking that we will eventually come to appreciate Wilde: above all, the necessity that compelled him to deride public opinion to the utmost at the same time that he made himself into its empty symbol and sacrificial lamb. He was a kind of Anglo-Irish Karl Kraus,[11] Benjamin might have said, working to discredit society as the middle classes of his time knew it in order to introduce a more creditable society: "the monster stands among us as the messenger of a more real humanism."[12]

In terms of the life and work of Wilde, a "more real humanism" might be one in which the overcoming of the inherited opposition of the aesthetic and the ethical did not exile the monster. For Wilde's involvement in his famous libel action, which revolves about the concept of written truth, was partly a function of his half-conscious vulnerability to the problem of "truth in art" and his need to put it to the test. Wilde was at an impasse on this question, having taken it as far as he could in *The Picture of Dorian Gray*, the critical dialogues, and the plays. As if his fate "cried out" to him from the edge of darkness, he turned in reckless resolve toward the courtroom as a new arena in which to discover himself. This philosophical imperative once taken into account, inimical as it may be to commonsensical notions of how to live one's life, we arrive at a view of his legal action as less of a blunder or piece of suicidal overreaching—one making him (as he well knew) into a kind of clown of history—than as the initiatory and indeed sacrificial event that led directly to his most original achievement, his theologically imbued autobiography *De Profundis*. As Wilde himself suggested while in prison, there are no easy answers to the problems his life poses for us: "And if life be, as it surely is, a problem to me, I am no less a problem to life" (*DP* 199).

Preface

One reason life was a "problem" to Wilde was that he neglected to formulate a philosophy of evil. As W. H. Auden suggested years ago, until Wilde was locked up in Reading Gaol, he looked upon British society merely as a great Lady Bracknell, comic and defeatable. Without a conception of active evil, Wilde could not bring himself to punish any of the characters in his comedies, and he returned obsessively in both ballad and in his life to the irremediable fact that the man he loved had ruined him and that "each man kills the thing he loves." Adopting Plato's view (and Plato's irony) that evil is essentially error, the imprisoned artist wrote *De Profundis* with a view toward educating the person who had wrecked his life. There is no evidence that he succeeded in his mission.

Critical commentary on Wilde is filled with impatience at his failure to formulate a more "practical" ethic. Roditi writes,

> [Wilde's] way of life requires, to justify it, an ethic which [he himself] had neglected to formulate. He might have chosen an ethic of predestination or privation of grace, such as the Jansenist ethic of Racine's *Phèdre* or of the Abbé Prévost's *Manon Lescaut*; or one of self-degradation and redemption through a descent into the deepest inferno of sin, such as that of Baudelaire or Dostoievsky; or a Satanic or dionysiac ethics, as in the philosophies of Stirner or Nietzsche at their lower levels of interpretation, where the expression of a super-man's personality justifies in itself all its possible effects on others; or a cynically hedonistic or a mechanistic or materialist ethics, such as that which the Marquis de Sade had borrowed from the *Système de la Nature* of Holbach and illustrated in the philosophic novel *Aline et Valcour*, where pleasure or self-knowledge through pleasure are all that matter.[13]

Roditi writes as if living were a matter of sorting through clearly defined options; his considerable learning seems to fail him in this passage in a way that Wilde's never did. For Wilde was not interested in systematizing but in "improvising" his life, in the primary sense of the verb *to improvise*: to see before, to compose through anticipation, as a great jazz musician improvises—calculated and spontaneous—from the depths of knowledge. In 1883 Wilde urged the art students of the Royal Academy to "realise completely your age in order completely to abstract yourself from it" (*M* 313). "To realise the nineteenth century," he would write later, "one must realise every century that has preceded it and that has contributed to its making" (*I* 178). How we view Wilde's achievement would accordingly have everything to do with our relative distance from ourselves—a divinatory distance, if you will. To those who aim to improvise, life may indeed be a "problem." But then, as Wilde's aphorism suggests, it is not entirely clear whether this is due to life as given to us or to those who choose to play with living. In the first chapter of this book, we look through the problems that life posed for Wilde into those that his life poses for us.

§ Cosmopolitan Criticism

1

❦ Wilde's Play-Drive and "the Still More Difficult Art of Living"

> For . . . [man] is only fully a human being when he plays. This propo-
> sition, which at the moment may sound like a paradox, . . . will, I
> promise you, prove capable of bearing the whole edifice of the art of
> the beautiful, and of the still more difficult art of living.
> —Schiller, *On the Aesthetic Education of Man*

Life and Art

OSCAR WILDE's philosophy of art developed over a period of some thirty years, although his writings on the subject scarcely span a decade. As a student at Portora Royal School in Dublin in the late 1860s, the young Wilde would assume the attitudes of holy figures on stained-glass windows to amuse his friends. Even as a boy, he understood intuitively what he would have later learned from reading Friedrich Schiller: the relations between art and life are to be understood primarily in terms of play.

As Wilde matured, so did this allusive playfulness, becoming at last the catalyst to his most somber art, as to that "still more difficult art of living." Writing *De Profundis* in prison, he would struggle to "realize his life," by which he meant both to discover and to create its form. Hovering over his life, as it were, in that condition of "utter repose and supreme agitation"[1] which Schiller identifies as the aesthetic state, Wilde nearly achieved the interpenetration of form and reality for which he had so long aimed. There in his radical solitude he momentarily formalized for all time the seemingly disastrous misjudgments leading up to the trials and the ensuing misery of prison life, making of misjudgment and misery a compositional necessity. Failure and success had become mutually determining conditions of artistic creation.

Viewed from the perspective of *De Profundis*, Wilde's life takes on a dynamic unity and sense of purpose precisely because of its shattered intentions. Wilde's role as a professional writer, his homosexuality, his devotion to his mother and friendship with his wife, his wide sense of citizenship, his decision to go to trial, his truncated relations with his sons, his imprisonment, his existence as outcast—all figure in the evolution of his identity as elements of an art: the art of his life. We might say that his overriding problem was to remain faithful to his life, severely damaged as it was, without betraying his art and, conversely, to maintain the integrity of his art without betraying the life. The strain of artificiality in *De Profundis*, something which critics have often pointed to with distaste,[2] runs deeply through its prose, and with good reason. Wilde self-consciously displays the transcendent "lie" of art, a lie that deserves to be defended if only because it corrects the far more pervasive and dangerous illusion that *things as they are* represent the whole truth.[3] Things *as they might have been, as they once were,* and *as they might be* figure in Wilde's ethical-aesthetic meditation on his life as well. Whatever may be said of Wilde's intentions, then, "escape" from life through art was not one of them, for art was to Wilde the sole condition that made life intelligible.

The inner logic of these contradictions may be brought to light in some degree by a consideration of Wilde's use of the words *art* and *life* themselves, which he simultaneously relates and distinguishes—as does Schiller—setting up a connection without either fusing or confusing the two. By *art*, Wilde means both the work of art and the aesthetic sense or potential in each of us. By *life*—which often appears in close proximity to the word *art*—Wilde means the ongoing experiences that constitute existence and, as such, contrast with the achieved stillness of artworks. That these experiences may include the apprehension or creation of art does not efface the distinction, dwelt upon throughout Wilde's life and work, between the finished work of art and lived experience.

Wilde's lifelong preoccupation with the difference between art and life is evidence of his compulsion to overcome it, and indeed the compulsion is evidence of his awareness of the difference. Even in his most idealized statements on art in general, or on the relations among the arts, Wilde rarely neglects to make some reference to their reception in life: "For there are not many arts, but one art merely—poem, picture, and Parthenon, sonnet and statue—all are in their essence the same, and *he who knows one, knows all*" (*M* 66, emphasis added). And when Wilde writes that "It is through Art, and through Art only, that we can realise our perfection; through

Art, and through Art only, that we can shield ourselves from the sordid perils of actual existence" (*I* 174), he uses *Art* to mean both the work we may read, see, or hear and the aesthetic capacity in each of us, which may enable an appreciation of the meaning not only of particular works of art but of "life" as well, in its actual sordid separateness from art.

It is a mark of Wilde's slipperiness, but also of his sanity, that these key words *art* and *life* are simultaneously linked and counterposed. This equivocation, moreover, is a consequence of Wilde's debt to his predecessors: nearly all the great Victorian prose writers who came before Wilde—Thomas Carlyle, John Ruskin, John Henry Newman, John Stuart Mill, and Matthew Arnold—were caught in a dualism that, however different the language in which it is cast, entailed a disabling opposition between an aesthetic principle and an ethical one. In each of these writers, that is, the intermittent qualities of the aesthetic (perception, spirit, spontaneity, inwardness) are set off against those marking the actions and responsibilities of beings who live in the world, and who obey the imperative to order the ongoing experiences that Wilde called "life." Ruskin and Newman sought to overcome this opposition by recourse to Christian doctrine, thus serving as a model for Wilde's own attempt to overcome it, however much Wilde diverged from their more conventional religious commitments. The spiritual and intellectual crises of these, as well as of the other prose writers mentioned, may be traced to a more or less openly acknowledged sense of helplessness before this philosophical opposition.

I elaborate on these arguments in chapter 2; the point here is that Wilde is much closer to the thought of these writers, even as he advances beyond them into new philosophical territory, than he is to that of his most frequently cited predecessor, Walter Pater. For Pater completely collapsed the distinction between "art" and "life" when, in his famous conclusion to *The Renaissance*, he placed art in the domain of sensations. Our sense experiences through art are of a higher—but not essentially *different*—quality than those of other sensations.

We note the Platonic provenance of Wilde's definition of art as a single imaginative principle: "For there are not many arts, but one art merely." In *The Renaissance*, Pater emphasizes the distinguishing sensuous features among the different arts, arguing (in his empiricism) against the existence of a single imaginative principle that can

3

be translated into the different languages of painting, music, poetry, and sculpture. Although Wilde would have agreed with Pater that the aesthetic critic should attend to these sensuous particulars, the fundamental principles of his criticism are not empirical and therefore are much farther from those of Pater than is generally supposed. It may be said that Wilde's first achievement was to retrieve Pater's "aesthetic moment" from exclusive absorption in the world of sensation, which was something that Pater, in his aversion to theory, could not do.[4]

In this discrimination, however, Wilde found himself confronted with the great encompassing problem of his career and of his life: that of reconnecting art and life on a new basis, or on a basis in which the differences between art and other "sensations" are preserved, but preserved in a way that does not lead back to the Victorian opposition between art and life, or aesthetics and ethics, or beauty and truth. Wilde accomplished this task, as I have already suggested, primarily in two ways: through the concept of "cosmopolitan criticism" and by the tactic of making one's *life* into a work of art. The aesthetic potential in each of us is strictly detachable from the work of art and so can be placed in the service of something other than creating art in the conventional sense: it can be placed in the service of criticism, which in Wilde is a form of aesthetic contemplation with worldly benefits; and, finally, it can be placed in the service of one's "life."

All of the major decisions of Wilde's career, therefore, above all those that led to his imprisonment, have everything to do with the linguistic and philosophical perplexities touched upon here; this is demonstrated more fully in chapter 4, "Wilde's Philosophy of Art." Chapter 2 assesses the impact that Wilde's predecessors had on his development of a "cosmopolitan criticism," and chapter 3 elaborates the ethical implications of his aestheticism.

I begin with a discussion of Wilde's life, for it is the life that has led most readers to assume that no "ideal" of any sort could possibly be associated with it. The traditional view, reinforced by Richard Ellmann's biography, conceives the story of Wilde's imprisonment and its aftermath as a messy personal misfortune of tragic proportions. More recent studies, as I have noted, present Wilde as the "epitome of the new type of professional writer,"[5] consciously promoting himself even after his imprisonment. Neither position is adequate to Wilde's artistic sense of his own life as it unfolded over the years, and neither can begin to deal with the culminating expression of this sense of life in *De Profundis.*

Aesthetic Fate

In Paris, after his release from prison, Wilde told the following story to Gustave Le Rouge:

> There was a time in my life when I had really nothing more to wish for. I was rich, held in great affection, famous, and in perfect health. At the time I was resting at Sorrento in a delightful villa whose garden was filled with orange trees. The sea lapped at the base of the terrace. From it my eye could follow the delightful, undulating curves of a countryside as sensuous as the body of a young girl.
>
> On this terrace I was absentmindedly contemplating the white sails which studded the sea at its horizon. Suddenly I began to reflect, with a secret feeling of terror, that in reality I was too happy, that such improbable bliss could only be a trap set by my evil genius. For a long time this idea haunted me.
>
> In the end I recalled the adventure of that tyrant of antiquity—Polycrates I think was his name—who had thrown a highly esteemed precious ring into the sea to ward off misfortune.
>
> I resolved to imitate Polycrates. It's true that his sacrifice had proved vain, but perhaps I would prove more fortunate. As far out into the sea as I could I flung a ring with a huge diamond that I kept in memory of a very dear friend. I thought I had appeased the hostile gods with this sacrifice and I regained my composure.

In his reminiscence, Le Rouge took note of the complete lack of bitterness and "air of indifference" with which Wilde related such anecdotes about himself, as though "he might have been referring to some other person."[6]

This little-known anecdote shows us the degree to which Wilde could summon an artistic distance on himself, composing the events of his life in terms of history and myth, as though these events were themselves foreign to him. So artfully disingenuous a relation to oneself may itself have invoked the "hostile Gods" of disaster, but to Wilde this relation was primarily a matter of aesthetics, although an aesthetics developed over the years out of wide-ranging studies in history, philosophy, and science. That it was also self-consciously tragic in character was, to Wilde, of secondary significance. In *De Profundis* Wilde writes of the "inevitableness" that characterizes the work of art. In viewing his own life as an evolving work of art, he aimed to realize not merely the meaning of that life, as he states in "The Critic as Artist," but "the collective life of the race. . . . For he to whom the present is the only thing that is present, knows nothing of the age in which he lives. To realise the nineteenth century, one must realise every century that has preceded it and that has contributed to its making" (*I* 178). To Wilde, who at Oxford had worked out an idealist interpretation of evolution,[7] fate was not simply a synonym for personal destiny; he understood it more broadly as the *fulfillment* of certain historical and mythic forces.[8] And here was the link with his conception of art: "Every single work of art is the fulfillment of a prophecy. For every work of art is the conversion of an idea into an image. Every single human being should be the fulfillment of a prophecy. For every human being should be the realisation of some ideal" (*DP* 210). Fate in Wilde is thus: the inevitability of the *work*, the working out of some prophetic idea, the realization of some historical potential.

Although Wilde was able to achieve such divinatory distance from himself only after he was sent to prison, his final exclusion from bourgeois society was not the sole occasion for this triumph. Wilde was the child of worldly, unconventional parents, and his investment in the bourgeois culture he would oppose was never very great. Jane Elgee Wilde, his mother, was a nationalist poet and translator from the French and German and his father William a distinguished surgeon, amateur archaeologist, and folklorist whose research on Irish folklore would influence Yeats. Before his marriage, Sir William Wilde fathered three illegitimate children, and during his marriage the extended family, legitimate and illegitimate children alike, summered together in Glenmainais, south of Dublin. Ellmann, Wilde's biographer, accounts for the tolerance of the illegitimate children by suggesting that in the Dublin of the time, "the old Regency permissiveness lingered."[9] There was also, however, a new urbanity, a lack of identification on the part of the Wildes with any specific living community. To the Wildes, there was the literary Ireland of the far-distant past and a political Ireland of the foreseeable future; they made their abode in a cosmopolitan present.

Not surprisingly, Wilde was early drawn to the transnational tenets of aestheticism, even before he went up to Oxford; what is not so well appreciated is that he came to aestheticism by way of ancient Greek literature. At Trinity College, Dublin, which he attended before moving to England, Wilde's favorite reading was Algernon Swinburne. His own translations of Euripides would show that poet's influence. In his last year at Trinity, the first volume of J. A. Symonds's *Studies in the Greek Poets* appeared, a work which conspicuously related contemporary aestheticism to the Greeks. Wilde was so impressed with this book that he began a correspondence with Symonds. As a scholar of Greek, Wilde had distinguished himself at Portora and Trinity, and he would go on to take a first-class degree in classics at Oxford in 1878. His knowledge of Greek culture is the foundation of what we may call his aesthetic politics; characteristically enough, in other words, his modernism has an archaic inspiration. "The Greeks were essentially a nation of artists," Symonds remarked to Wilde,[10] identifying a comprehensive *political* possibility that Wilde would develop later in "The Soul of Man under Socialism" and in the cosmopolitan aestheticism of "The Critic as Artist."

Wilde studied the classics at Trinity College under J. P. Mahaffy, a Kantian idealist who had an interest in the materialist historian, H. T. Buckle, an interest that prompted him to look for ways to reconcile materialist and idealist theories of civilized history. Mahaffy included Wilde on trips to Italy in 1875 and to Greece in 1877, and, as the editors of the *Oxford Notebooks* suggest, he prepared Wilde for the first major philosophical-linguistic influence he was to encounter at Oxford: that of the philologist F. Max Müller. It was under Müller that "Wilde learned of the possibility of reconciling evolutionary science with philosophical idealism".[11] Not published until 1989, the notes and Commonplace Book that Wilde kept at Oxford are singularly lacking in references to blue china and gray silk shirts; they bear out the truth of the editors' statement that the "most important influences from [the Oxford] program of study came in philosophy" (*ON* 8).

Unlike Mahaffy, who as a member of the Church of England sought a via media in the controversies of matter and mind, German-educated Müller attempted a genuine merging of "ruthless skepticism and . . . vivid imagination" (*ON* 8)—qualities that Müller claimed were combined in great historians and that also characterize Wilde's critical writing. Although his conclusions were ultimately dismissed by scientific linguistics, Müller's wide-ranging attempts to reconcile his idiosyncratic idealism with newly refurbished theories of racial-linguistic inheritance greatly impressed Oscar

Wilde, who would later insist that language is "the parent, and not the child, of thought" (*I* 132). It was within the philosophical context of Müller's thought, with whom he studied during his first year, that Wilde was able to absorb the most decisive personal influences on the development of his aestheticism: those of his other Oxford teachers, John Ruskin and Walter Pater. It may well be that only the impact of Müller's learned and venturesome formulations on Wilde's youthful imagination could have made it possible for him to be equally receptive to Pater's empiricism and Ruskin's idealism. As the *Notebooks* plainly show, Wilde was not drifting with every intellectual current, but was carefully developing the philosophical framework by which to make sense of a confluence of contradictory forces.

Ruskin's influence would prove to be the greater over time.[12] Then Slade Professor of Fine Arts, Ruskin was a lecturer of extraordinary power, unlike the quiet and rather stiff Pater, whose prose style Wilde would later criticize for its lack of vital rhythm. Wilde did not attend Pater's lectures but was in regular attendance at Ruskin's on Florentine art. He also participated in Ruskin's road-building experiment in which the professor supervised a group of sleepy undergraduates in the early-morning communal task of improving a road. It may be, as Ellmann writes, that this experiment "fostered Wilde's conviction that art had a role to play in the improvement of society,"[13] but it probably also fostered some skepticism toward the naive meliorism therein exhibited. The project lasted a few months until the wealthy Ruskin left for Venice, after which the road slowly sank out of sight. The absurdity of the scheme could not have been lost on Wilde, whose utopian tendencies were informed by a philosophical and theological irony.

Wilde and Ruskin saw each other often and admired as well as liked one another.[14] (Pater, on the other hand, complained of Wilde's "vulgarity." "You have a phrase for everything," he said to Wilde reprovingly.) Questions of morality played a major role in Ruskin's aesthetic, as they would in that of his disciple. And Wilde's cosmopolitan inclinations were nourished by exposure to the sheer breadth of Ruskin's comprehension of European art. In Proust's words, Ruskin "realized . . . the dream of the great popes of the Middle Ages: [namely,] 'Christian Europe.' . . . [He] could pass thus from one country to another, for the same soul he had adored in the stones of Pisa was also the one that had given to the stones of

Chartres their immortal form. No one has felt as he did the unity of Christian art during the Middle Ages."[15] Only a few years later on lecture-tour in America, Wilde would repeatedly stress the power of art to create "a common intellectual atmosphere between all countries" (*M* 268).

Wilde's rejection of a puritanical Christian ethic may have been a consequence of his association with Ruskin as well. He knew of Ruskin's unconsummated, annulled marriage, and he may also have known of Ruskin's obsession with the child Rose La Touche. In his lectures and writings, Ruskin tirelessly proclaimed the psychic advantages to be gained by renouncing sensual gratification in the manner of a medieval Christian saint, and he exhorted his audience to marry the life of the spirit to art. In a lecture at Oxford, he once interrupted an especially passionate exposition of a picture to make an all-out appeal to his listeners to fall in love at the first opportunity. The charm and the power of such demonstrations no doubt affected Wilde—he echoes Ruskin's judgments concerning the spiritual in art as late as *De Profundis*, where he returns to Ruskin's preference for the Gothic—but neither could he miss the irony of their coming from a man believed to be impotent. "It is enough that our fathers believed," writes Wilde in "The Critic as Artist." "They have exhausted the faith-faculty of the species" (*I* 177).

Between Wilde and Pater there was more of a mutual influence at work. Wilde was not so much in awe of Pater as he was of Ruskin, and he spoke more in Pater's presence. "Fortunately for me he could not talk at all," Wilde said to Frank Harris. The moribund timidity of Pater made him a less attractive presence to Wilde.[17] When Pater died, Wilde commented: "Was he ever alive?" Pater's homosexuality was so thoroughly circumscribed by Victorian culture that it manifested itself, in the form of a central motif of male friendship, across six centuries of art and literature in Pater's criticism. The theme of male friendship would be developed far more variously in Wilde's writing, particularly in *The Picture of Dorian Gray* and "The Portrait of Mr. W. H.," both philosophical investigations of the anxiety of influence. More withdrawn and repressed than Wilde, Pater was no model for Wilde as a man. Through association with Pater as well as Ruskin, the ethical aspect of aestheticism—the question of how to live one's life, the possibility of living it aesthetically—first clarified itself for him, but Wilde had in mind at this point an active life in the world, not academic seclusion at

Oxford. Living aesthetically meant, among other things, making a living at it. Partly because of his own material circumstances, Wilde would develop a more vigorous form of criticism than Pater ever did, one conscious of the sociological realities pressing in upon art, as upon those who live by and for it.

Wilde was from the beginning aware of both the grandiosity of his ambition to make his life into art and the possible commercial value of such a venture, as is revealed in his parody of his own aesthetic stance, which he engineered through his dandiacal dress and the self-mocking exaggerations of his speech. By the time of his skillfully marketed tour of America in 1882, during which his playful narcissism reached its height, he was the publicist more than the practitioner of the cult of art-for-art's-sake. Cultivating "posing," he kept his distance from the cult. In his essays, dialogues, and plays, Wilde was working towards the deeply meditated aestheticism of "The Soul of Man under Socialism," "The Critic as Artist," and *De Profundis*, in which laws of conduct and faith in supernatural revelation are tested against the undeniably dangerous powers of *aesthesis*. His early self-parody, which faded with his dandy's dress, was a function of this ambition, this desire for an audience. Wilde understood early that certain stylish brands of fin-de-siècle aestheticism bespoke a reaction against the emergent consumer capitalism, as well as the strangest of capitulations to it, and he was willing to exploit the paradox in his own person. He said to Frank Harris, "Every time my name is mentioned in a paper, I write at once to admit that I am the Messiah. Why is Pears' soap successful? Not because it is better or cheaper than any other soap, but because it is more strenuously puffed. The journalist is my 'John the Baptist.' "[18]

As recent studies have shown, Wilde's incipient homosexuality played a role in these developments within his thought and character, although how great a role is difficult to determine.[19] According to Wilde's biographers, he did not become actively homosexual at Oxford, though he was well-acquainted with the group of young men surrounding Pater. When, at the age of thirty-two, and after having married, he was initiated into homosexual experience by Robert Ross, there is little evidence that he suffered guilt. Identifying himself above all as an artist, and at home in the artistic, bohemian, and aristocratic circles he had known since childhood, circles in which homosexuality was not a pressing concern let alone the guilt-ridden bogey it was to the middle classes, the cosmopolitan Wilde exhibits little of that anxiety on the subject of homosexuality that others of his generation felt.[20]

When Wilde's sexuality fully unfolded, it was ferocious and unashamed, as Ellmann has amply shown. If in Nietzsche's words, "the degree and the type of a man's sexuality reaches to the highest peaks of his spirit" (*BG* 74), the analogy to Wilde's sexuality in his art may be seen in the strain of metaphysical-moral anarchy. In the plays, for example, Wilde repeatedly throws into question all assurance of a continuous personal identity. Images of split and half-hidden selves in *Dorian Gray* and *The Importance of Being Earnest* may be seen as metaphors for sexual difference, as long as one bears in mind that no essential identity is being promoted as a last resort. As in Carlyle's *Sartor Resartus*, identity is always "clothed" or masked in Wilde's writings; it is as much a relating *to* oneself as a thing in itself.[21] When Wilde does write of identity in *De Profundis*, he moves beyond subjectivist psychology toward a metaphysical conception associated with art and memory.[22] The "spiritual singularity of artists sets them socially apart, in the long run, whether they are sexual 'outsiders' or not," writes Helen Vendler.[23] In *De Profundis* it is the "spiritual singularity" that Wilde is interested in understanding, intensified as it no doubt was by his "deviancy."

If Robert Sherard's account of Wilde's words to him on his wedding trip to Paris is to be trusted,[24] Wilde's marriage to Constance Lloyd was not unsatisfying to him; and we know that he wanted to return to his wife after his release from prison. This suggests that Wilde may have made a conscious choice to exploit a predisposition towards homosexuality. According to Alick West, he may have done so "because he thus expressed more easily than by the labour of thought the antagonism between himself and the social system." To West, this move was compensatory: "He went into the underworld to live what he had not written. He had not put into his plays more than a part of the intellectual [and revolutionary] content of his other writings."[25] But if Wilde saw his life as a work of art, his entrance into the underworld, as he implies in *De Profundis*, justified itself; it does so for posterity in the work itself.

Wilde's catastrophic relations with Alfred Douglas, at any rate, would prove to be the undoing of Wilde's original ambition to make his life into art, as well as the condition for its ultimate fulfillment in *e Profundis*. Wilde first met Douglas at the age of thirty-six, just as his literary genius was crystallizing. Wilde's *Poems*, published ten years earlier, were derivative and undeveloped. They show an artist and thinker in a state of oscillation, such as itself would receive ingenious expression in the multigeneric "Portrait of Mr. W. H.," a short story, mystery, and work of literary criticism all in one. Oscar Browning acutely observed of the poems "the irregular pulsations of a sympathy that never wearies. Roman Catholic ritual, stern Puritanism, parched Greek islands, cool English lanes and streams, Paganism and Christianity, despotism and Republicanism, Wordsworth, Milton, and Mr Swinburne, receive in turn the same passionate devotion."[26] But with *The Picture of Dorian Gray* and *Intentions*, both published the year he met Douglas, Wilde discovered his critical genius and began the plays that would result in his theatrical masterpiece, *The Importance of Being Earnest*. As Wilde entered the phase of his most intense definition and discipline as an artist, then, he fell in love with a man who was very much his opposite: infantile, rapacious, and idle. One reason for Wilde's taking up with Douglas may have been that Douglas represented that primitive brutality and physical violence that Wilde—with his "dominating self-possession," as Yeats described it, his " 'cold scientific intellect,' " as Lionel Johnson observed,[27] and his critical, detached sensibility—had risen above. "They were an extraordinary pair and were complementary in a hundred ways, not only in mind, but in character," wrote Frank Harris.[28]

Steeped as he was in the conventions of Greek life,[29] Wilde saw in his relations with the young man, who also had published poetry, the promise of the "hearer/inspirer" dynamic of Platonic love. Instead, he found himself increasingly fearful both of the violence in Douglas's character and his own inexplicable vulnerability to Douglas's demands. "He frightened me, Frank, as much as he attracted me," Wilde said to Frank Harris, "and I held away from him. But he wouldn't have it; he sought me out again and again and I couldn't resist him."[30] The pathology of the relationship is explored in *Salomé*, where Herod, who together with John the Baptist represents Wilde, offers Salomé half his kingdom to dance before him. Wilde offered Douglas nearly everything—his time, money, and devotion, his support as a fellow poet and his sympathy as an older and wiser friend—but that was not enough for Douglas, who would be satisfied with nothing less than Wilde's "entire existence."

When Herod first encounters Salomé, he is not made suspicious by her frightening self-sufficiency. He offers her drink and she replies, "I am not thirsty, Tetrarch." He offers her food and she replies, "I am not hungry, Tetrarch." He offers her a chair to sit down and she replies, "I am not tired, Tetrarch."[31] She wants only one thing. Through all of Douglas's arrogant histrionics—his tantruming self-pity, his self-righteous pleas for forgiveness—it is evident he could feel no real remorse for what happened to Wilde. He too only wanted one thing, and he got it. As Wilde writes, "Having made your own of my genius, my will power and my fortune, you required, in the blindness of an inexhaustible greed, my entire existence. You took it" (*DP* 158). In *De Profundis*, however, Wilde's knowledge of his own part in the tragedy had deepened: "And that I may not spare myself any more than you I will add this: that dangerous to me as my meeting with you was, it was rendered fatal to me by the particular moment in which we met. For you were at that time of life when all that one does is no more than the sowing of the seed, and I was at that time of life when all that one does is no less than the reaping of the harvest" (234). The disastrous course of the relationship was not simply a function of Wilde's failure of will, but of a pathological need on Douglas's part to demand everything from one whose tendency it was to give, and whose capacity or "harvest" was at this stage in his life at its most abundant.

In the end, Wilde would cast the relationship with Douglas not in terms derived from Plato but those borrowed from Robert Louis Stevenson. In *The Strange Case of Dr. Jekyl and Mr. Hyde* (1886), a work Wilde knew well, it is Jekyl who creates Hyde out of himself and then suffers the consequences. Like Hyde, Douglas made greater and greater claims on Wilde's life. His sudden and surprising appearances, his "low stature" and "undisciplined and untutored nature," his irresponsible demands and promiscuous character, the "utter horror" he arouses in Wilde when he becomes physically violent, the sense of being "polluted," "soiled," and "shamed" by the association—all the details down to the "twitch and gesture of [his] nervous hands" echo the portrait of Hyde. Wilde calls Douglas "my shadow"—as Jekyl calls Hyde—an inextricable part of his ethical being operating to destroy him from within (166–73).

Having never made an absolute separation between "art" and "life," and being unwilling to sacrifice any aspect of his life to the demands of his art, Wilde was unusually receptive to experience.

Harris observed, "The truth is that [Wilde's] extraordinarily receptive mind went with an even more abnormal receptivity of character: unlike most men of marked ability, he took colour from his associates."[32] As if he too had been reading *Dr. Jekyl and Mr. Hyde*, Harris emphasizes Wilde's failure to resist the changes Douglas was working on his character, and he takes note of his decline (around 1894): "Without knowing the cause the change in Oscar astonished me again and again."[33] And "He changed greatly and for the worse: he was growing coarser and harder every year. All his friends noticed this. Even M. André Gide, who was a great admirer . . . was compelled to deplore his deterioration. He says: 'One felt there was less tenderness in his looks, and there was something harsh in his laughter, and a wild madness in his joy. . . . He had grown reckless, hardened and conceited.' "[34] Yet Wilde could not shake Douglas: "I could not get rid of you out of my life. I had tried it again and again" (*DP* 176).

Douglas's crime, as is Hyde's, is lack of responsibility: "you gambled with my life, as you gambled with my money, carelessly, recklessly, indifferent to the consequences" (174); "whatever you did was to be paid for by someone else; I don't mean merely in the financial sense . . . but in the broadest, fullest sense of transferred responsibility" (226). Jekyl pays for Hyde's crimes, just as Wilde would be convicted for acts that Douglas and others committed: "The sins of another were being placed to my account. Had I so chosen, I could on either trial have saved myself" (180). Douglas was in fact what the court believed Wilde to be: incurably promiscuous and a corruptor of youth. In *De Profundis* Wilde describes his Jekyl-like vulnerability to Douglas each time the latter returns to him with stories and excuses, begging forgiveness. Wilde's generous temperament, his relaxed and playful susceptibility—in short, his artistic imagination—gave him no immunity against such narratives, whereas Douglas was impervious to Wilde's influence: "Of all the people who have ever crossed my life you were the one, and the only one, I was unable in any way to influence in any direction" (228). In "The Portrait of Mr. W. H.," another meditation on questions of susceptibility, influence, and immunity, Wilde writes of the "reality of loss" that comes about with the "transference of personality" worked by influence: "Every disciple takes away something from his master."[35]

In this strange psychodynamic, it was as if Douglas were a part of Wilde's deep-lying self, depleting him from within: a grotesque parody of the ancient image of male comradeship that dominated the work of Wilde's teacher, Walter Pater, and the dead end to the theme of influence that Wilde had begun exploring in *Dorian Gray* and "The Portrait of Mr. W. H." Wilde writes bitterly of male friendship in *De Profundis*, in the section on Rosencrantz and Guildenstern: "They are what modern life has contributed to the antique ideal of friendship" (233). Yet, as Linda Dowling has shown, the final aim of Wilde's communication to Douglas was "to restore the true relations of older lover and younger beloved, *erastes* and *eromenos*, which had been so inverted in their actual friendship, returning it to the 'hearer/inspirer' dyad of Dorian and Platonic love."[36] In *De Profundis*, Wilde recovered the pattern of his life's artistic significance, the key to which was the identity between moral and aesthetic beauty, that both Douglas and prison had almost taken from him.

How did Wilde manage to do this? Despite the painful, degrading intimacy into which Wilde had permitted Douglas to draw him, much of his moral freedom was intact. Wilde's friendship with his wife remained constant. Unconventional in her tolerance of Wilde's living habits from the beginning of their marriage, Constance Wilde proved to be a genuine solace to him through the trials and for some time after. When Wilde was in prison, she traveled in ill health from Genoa to Reading to break the news of his mother's death to him in person. Not simply above petty vindictiveness, she was as actively generous as Wilde himself. Instances of spontaneous charity, as opposed to the calculated philanthropy of the age, abound in the biographies of Wilde. Such acts gave pleasure and assistance to many who barely acknowledged his existence after the trials, even to some who assisted in his prosecution. Like his parents, who were also involved in a libel suit, Wilde invited envy for the very reason that he was oblivious to it. Many of the most damning clues in the case against Wilde were provided by an entirely voluntary agent, an actor named Charles Brookfield. When Wilde learned of Brookfield's role in his prosecution, he could say only "How absurd of Brookfield!"[37] Wilde's character in this respect remained steady throughout the trials. He maintained a magnanimity and lack of malice despite the fact that many friends dropped him and few fellow artists signed petitions for mitigation of a sentence that was widely known to result in death.

Wilde's efforts on behalf of imprisoned children, "when set against the system, leaves no question as to Wilde's moral superiority over the society that condemned him" writes G. Wilson Knight.[38] Knight refers to Wilde's letters to the *Daily Chronicle* on the subject of jailed children, but Wilde's scrawled note about freeing children incarcerated near his own cell, which he pushed under the door for Warder Martin, has survived as well: "Please find out for me the name of A.2.11. Also: the names of the children who are in for the rabbits; and the amount of the fine. . . . Can I pay this and get them out? If so I will get them out tomorrow. Please dear friend do this for me."[39]

Wilde made friends in prison and was often penalized for being found talking to other prisoners. His friendship with the warder, Thomas Martin, is recorded in the scraps of paper they exchanged. In a note of thanks to Martin, Wilde attributes his improved appearance to Martin's kindness toward him: "That is because I have a good friend who gives me the *Chronicle*, and *promises* me ginger biscuits! O.W." At the bottom of this note Martin wrote in pencil: "Your ungrateful I done more than promise."[40] That Wilde could inspire joking under such circumstances suggests the moral vigor of his presence, an energy in turn deriving from his aesthetic intelligence. For Wilde could rise above the mounting horrors of his existence—as surely as he could describe himself in *De Profundis* standing on the center platform of Clapham Junction in convict dress, handcuffed, surrounded by a jeering mob—precisely because of his artistic distance from himself, a distance that attained its peak, I have suggested, only after his disastrous relationship with Alfred Douglas had resulted in imprisonment.

For this reason, perhaps no moment of Wilde's life is more important to an understanding of both his fate and character than the moment, after the first trial, when he decided to remain in England rather than to escape to France, for at that moment he effectively chose prison. Much of what we know of Wilde's irregular manner of living in the period leading up to this decision—his restless travels and his rage for pleasures in Morocco and Paris, for example—would suggest the naturalness of his fleeing and living out the rest of his life in Paris. Indeed, for a time Wilde evinced the "prodigious oscillation" that Søren Kierkegaard noted as a trait of the aesthete, and a Hamlet-like indecision. A partially packed suitcase lay open on the bed of his room at the Cadogan Hotel, where he went to stay after Queensberry was acquitted. But as the moment of decision drew near, he seems to have given himself over to ideas of fate and play similar to those of Hamlet in the "If it be now . . ." speech of act 5, conscious of his responsibility to himself not to draw back in fear. He was surrounded by his Horatios, the great friends he had in Robert Ross and Frank Harris, who urged him to flee. But he chose to remain. As shown in chapter 4, Wilde may have been vulnerable to and driven to the courtroom for complex philosophical reasons. But the moral element in his decision at the Cadogan Hotel should not be overlooked: Wilde's resolve not to flee a situation he had played so large a part in creating, the determination to see a process through he himself had set in motion.

For Wilde had at last begun to *realize*—the central word in *De Profundis*—what he had done in seeking protection from a society whose laws he had been flouting, and, given his character, he was as unlikely to renege on that, or any, realization as to turn others in so as to escape punishment himself. (A month before the first trial, Wilde said to André Gide, "My friends advise me to be prudent. Prudent! How could I be that? It would mean going backward."[41]) Then and now, few have been able to consider his intentions except perhaps in psychoanalytic terms that portray him as one driven by unconscious guilt over his homosexuality. And few have been able to understand his confidence that he was making progress in this affair (rather than "going backward"). It would take a fellow artist like William Butler Yeats to see the moral singularity of the act. Years later, recalling his feelings at the time in his autobiography, Yeats wrote, "I was certain that, guilty or not guilty, he would prove himself a man. . . . I have never doubted, even for an instant, that he made the right decision."[42]

Because for Wilde the concept of fate was, from his early years, an aesthetic concept, the aesthetic itself possessed for him a manifestly ethical dimension. Wilde believed, in a fully classical manner, that we realize our potential as human beings by progressing from the realm of necessity or instinct to the realm of self-consciousness and freedom. The contemplative attitude (*theoria*), which was the basis of Aristotle's *Ethics* as Wilde understood it, is the means and end of self-perfection; and Friedrich Schiller's *Letters on Aesthetic Education*, which also influenced Wilde, assume that each individual man bears within himself the capacity for ideal manhood and that this ideal unity of spirit and nature, freedom and necessity, can be called into actual life only by "aesthetic education."

In a letter to Douglas, the educator Wilde tried to make the self-ish young man understand this; behind his effort to make Douglas both *see* and *contemplate* his life Wilde's entire philosophy of art and life resonates: "I have to write your life to you and you have to re-alise it. . . . Whatever is realised is right" (*DP* 177). Over a decade earlier in America, Wilde often quoted what William Morris had once said to him: "I have tried to make each of my workers an artist, and when I say an artist I mean a man" (*M* 275).

As B Follows A

The great expression in nineteenth-century philosophy of the dif-ferent alternatives facing Wilde from within may be found in Kierkegaard's *Either/Or*, first published in 1843, but not translated into English until 1944. Although Wilde could not have read it, it speaks to his predicament more than almost any other work, articu-lating at the level of individual choice the more abstract dualism Wilde inherited from his predecessors. In *Either/Or*, Kierkegaard lays out two contrasting philosophies of life: the aesthetic and the ethical. The aesthetic is represented by the views and convictions of a young romantic, designated A, the ethical by those of a married man, called Judge Wilhelm and designated B. The great problem that this work poses is virtually the same posed by Wilde's life as a whole: how to see these two alternative philosophies of life *together*, if not exactly as one; how to give one's "life" the meaning of "art."

Conceived in terms similar to those found in Pater and in Wilde's *The Picture of Dorian Gray*, the heart of the aesthetic life in Kierkegaard is the attempt to dwell wholly in the present. The ro-mantic lover, who is the paradigm of the aesthetic ideal, goes from one woman to another restlessly seeking "new sensations," a for-mula often found in Pater and Wilde. His goal is his own satisfac-tion; he seeks at all costs to avoid pain and boredom. Taking in through his senses the immediate world (the root of the word *aes-thesis* is to perceive), the aesthete "enters into relation only with the beautiful,"[43] not directly with human beings or with chronology. He has no sense of time (A gives no precise dates)—or, to word it an-other way, that is *all* he has. Gathering what he is, what he would be, into "one desperate effort to see and touch, [he] shall hardly have time to make theories about the things [he] see[s] and touch[es]," writes Pater in the conclusion of *The Renaissance*. He knows "an interval" and only an interval. He does not meditate the past for any practical purpose; he lives in the world of possibility. Reality is significant to him only as an occasion, as a stimulus; and, conscious that all stimuli exhaust themselves, he lives in despair, at times in madness, and his life is characterized by "prodigious oscillation." "Desire, at the end, was a malady, or a madness, or both," writes Wilde in *De Profundis*, "I grew careless of the lives of others. I took where it pleased me and passed on" (194).

In *Either/Or*, the paradigm of the ethical is the married man, or marriage itself, a state of commitment and obligation through time. If the aesthete "is" what he would be—the mask—the ethical man becomes what he is; he chooses himself or decides. He reflects on the past in order to refine his project for the future. The root of the word *ethic* is character; it has also been associated with an idea of *place*, suggesting the nearness of ethics to conceptions of home and nation. The ethical man exists in his relation to others, to institutions, and to time. He is *placed*, whereas the aesthete, in Pater's famous verb, *drifts*.

To the aesthete, conscience is only a higher—or perhaps lower—degree of consciousness. In *The Picture of Dorian Gray*, one of the last sensations Dorian seeks is morality,[44] just as Kierkegaard's seducer devises fine moral challenges to his prowess as a lover. Like Wilde, Kierkegaard's aesthete writes most brilliantly in aphorisms, the form most antithetical to any system of thought or intellectual "home" (as Giles Deleuze suggests). When Wilde made the acquaintance of Henry James in America, James remarked upon his own nostalgia for London. Wilde dodgily replied, "You care for places? The world is my home."[45] But the same Wilde made the most important ethical decision of his life in terms of place by choosing to remain in London rather than to run away, to retain rather than break his ties to a particular locus and situation, with all of the institutional responsibilities attached to them. And when courts pass sentences, as in the case of Wilde, the punishment is to force the most intense form of "ethical" existence: to remain in a particular place for a particular period of time.

In *De Profundis* Wilde adopted the characteristic form of Kierkegaard's ethical man: the letter. The paradigm of ethical consciousness is the letter because by definition it realizes a connection to another. In *Either/Or* the aim of Judge Wilhelm's letters is pedagogic, just as *De Profundis* aims to educate Douglas in the significance of what has happened to them—"I have to write your life to you and you have to realise it" (177)—and to teach him how to live in the world. For example, Wilde instructs him as to how the first volume of poetry by a young poet should be presented. He concludes *De Profundis* with advice to Douglas on how he might receive the bitter content of his letter.

As Alastair MacIntyre points out, the disjunction between the ethical and the aesthetic in *Either/Or* is felt in the way the two arguments cannot meet, because Judge Wilhelm uses ethical criteria to judge between the ethical and the aesthetic, whereas A uses aesthetic criteria.[46] Yet Kierkegaard evidently wants us to grasp the arguments in conjunction—to do, in short, what Wilde attempted. The book "is not only *called Either/Or*," he wrote, "but it *is* Either/Or."[47] Paradoxically, it presents a *choice* in the form of a *single* proposition. For although the papers of A do not mention B, "the outlook of B is constantly in mind and is constantly protested against. In this way, B is present, though hidden, in A's papers, and A is present in every page that B has written."[48] In his mock-preface, the editor of *Either/Or* describes it as "the work of one man;" "he who says A must also say B." One follows upon the other. The author is "a man who had lived through both phases, or who had thought upon both."[49] In Kierkegaard's *Concluding Unscientific Postscript*, he emphasizes that the book offers "no result and no finite decision." "There is no didacticism in the book."[50] It provides no conclusion but transforms everything into inwardness.

As Kierkegaard writes in the mock-preface, he wanted to free the reader of all "finite questions."[51] We are not to attach ourselves to either philosophy in isolation from the other. We contemplate their separation in the abstract, but we live *through* both. In actual existence, the question of "either the aesthetic or the ethical" cannot be answered. Or, as Wilde writes in *De Profundis*, where he does resolve this problem, "We think in Eternity, but we move slowly through Time" (202–3). Our aesthetic powers and our ethical existence are both joined and disjoined. "To be entirely free, and at the same time entirely dominated by law, is the eternal paradox of human life that we realise every moment" (*DP* 172).

Just as Kierkegaard wanted to leave the reader with an abiding problem, an "existence in thought,"[52] rather than an abstract solu-

tion, so Wilde leaves us in a state of suspension beyond all problem-
solving: after his release from prison, he wrote, "I was a problem for
which there was no solution."[53] If Wilde's personal tragedy has any
ultimate meaning, it presumably must be traced in terms of the
problematical relation between ethics and aesthetics: we understand
them separately, but we live them in tandem. This is preferable to
trying to live them separately or to choosing one over the other, because *alone* each is inadequate. Were I to deal with each individually,
Kierkegaard's mock-editor implies, were I to ask each what he
thought about my publishing his papers, for example, "A would
probably interpose no objection to the publication; he would probably warn the reader: read them or refuse to read them, you will re-
gret both." Taken by himself, then, the aesthete is an utter nihilist,
indifferent as to whether he is read or not.

"What B would say is more difficult to decide. He would perhaps reproach me, especially with regard to the publication of A's
papers. He would let me feel that he had no part in them, that he
washed his hands of responsibility."[54] Taken by himself, the ethical
man only wants to censor A. And if he cannot do that, he cruelly ab-
rogates responsibility. The final choice, then, is not between nihilism on the one hand and unqualified condemnation on the other,
but between one or the other of these attitudes OR both of them
together.[55]

"To be entirely free, and at the same time entirely dominated by
law, is the eternal paradox of human life that we realise every moment," whether we are conscious of it or not. Once again: Wilde
uses the word *realize* here to mean *live out* or *make actual*. This is
what our existence *is*, in other words, whether we recognize it or
not. Like Kierkegaard's intertwined A and B, the aesthete is unable
to escape the ethical basis of life because he cannot transcend time
except purely in his imagination. He cannot deny the irrevocable
changes that take place over time in his life and character. He can
never repeat the same emotion (as Wilde writes in "The Critic as
Artist") and he can only protest his ties to others—his place of origin and his family—rather than free himself of them. Nor can the
ethical man escape the aesthetic basis of life any more than he can
refrain from taking in the immediate, sensuous present so as to
order it—or "wash his hands," as Judge Wilhelm would like to do,
of all ties to those aspects of life that *cannot* be readily subsumed
under ethical categories.

Placed within the walls of the prison and obliged to remain there for two long years, a slave of the calendar and of a system of regulations admitting of no exception, Wilde was as far from living the aesthetic ideal of pleasure in new and varied sensations as he could be. Or was he? He often said later that he "found his soul" in prison, and of course he wrote *De Profundis* there, a work in which he gave expression to every sensation of shame and sorrow that was new to him. Despite the cruel regimen, he still enjoyed the sight of "the black branches of the trees that show themselves above the prison walls and are so restless in the wind" (218). Three years later, ill and dying in Paris, Wilde uttered one of his most famous witticisms. Alluding to the ugly wallpaper in his hotel room, he mordantly remarked that he knew "one or the other of us would have to go"—which is to say that Art, even the bad Art of that wallpaper, will no doubt outlast Nature, my failing body. Wilde was an aesthete to the end, but he faced death with the resignation of a moralist. His inexpungeable sense of play held the two points of view in constant relation, as the "difficult art of living" became at last the necessity of dying.

2

✑ Wilde and His Predecessors

We Homeless Ones ... We children of the future, how could we be at
home in the present? We are unfavourable to all ideals which could
make us feel at home in this frail, broken-down, transition period.
—Nietzsche, *Joyful Wisdom*

Cosmopolitanism

THE ROOTS of the word *cosmopolitan*, as we know, are the Greek *kos-
mos*, world order, and *polites*, citizen, from *polis* or city. In turn, the
Indo-European root of *polis*, *pele*, suggests a citadel or fortified
place. The cosmopolitan says, "the cosmos is my polis," the world is
my home. Yet how can one feel at home within the vastness of the
world (especially if one inhabits a society as bourgeois and nationalistic as nineteenth-century England), let alone 'fortified' by such an
expanse? The idea seems mere puffery. Like Jack in *The Importance
of Being Earnest*, one may as well be born in a handbag in the cloak-
room of Victoria Station ("the Brighton line").

Furthermore, what would it mean to be a "citizen" of the
world? The cosmopolitan has a sense of entitlement and belonging
(wittily established by "the Brighton line") that we associate with
citizenship; yet he is by definition unencumbered. Ideally he owns
no property. ("In the interests of the rich we must get rid of it," says
Wilde of its burdens in "The Soul of Man under Socialism" [*I* 278].)
He belongs to the world and is at home there. Wilde himself was
literally at home everywhere from London to Leadville, Colorado,
and most at home in Paris, which would become the center of cosmopolitanism in the period immediately following Wilde's death
there in 1900. (Wilde was so at home in the French language, according to Gide, that he would pretend to hesitate for a word to
which he wanted to call his listeners' attention.) The opposite of the
provincial, although not necessarily of the patriot, the cosmopolitan

may be compared to the *nomad*, who is at home nowhere. Just as the archetypal cosmopolitan is Wilde, the archetypal nomad, as Deleuze suggests,[1] is Friedrich Nietzsche. Unlike the nomad, the cosmopolitan is a "citizen" and in that sense a *civilian*, not employed by the military or the police or any similar agent. To be so employed would be to negate his membership in the "world" because it would tie him to a particular government or nation. This transcendent "citizenliness" is essential to the character of the cosmopolitan. In Wilde, it is revealed in his active engagement in the artistic, intellectual, and social life that he encountered in his travels to London, Paris, and other European and American cities. Whereas the nomad acknowledges no immediate roots, the cosmopolitan lays down roots everywhere he goes. He makes himself at home, for however brief a stay.

It is part of the paradoxical existential condition of the cosmopolitan that he *has* roots, even "original" ones, though he is perpetually cut off from them. Like James Joyce, the cosmopolitan may have a passionate sense of the national or of national origin and of the local, but his first allegiance is to the world.[2] We know Wilde inherited from his parents an intense awareness of Irish national heritage. In the aftermath of the famine, and the Encumbered Estates Court sales of property, William Wilde built a villa on the shores of Lough Corrib, naming it Moytura after the legendary battle of the gods and aboriginal Irish.[3] He and Lady Wilde christened their son Oscar Fingal O'Flahertie Wilde. Growing up in Dublin, Wilde was familiar with the literary recovery of Celtic civilization by poets, antiquaries, and historians through his own parents who, as earlier mentioned, made significant contributions to it; it therefore comes as no surprise that Wilde later asserts that creative imagination is "the result of heredity," that it is "concentrated race experience" (*I* 181), etc. Out of this racial consciousness, however, Wilde did not embrace a provincial primitivism, but he developed a critical sensibility and a theory of the utmost importance of the critical spirit to the creative enterprise. Since Irish national identity (and English national identity, also) developed as part of a colonial relationship, Wilde decolonized himself when he gave himself to the cosmopolitan critical spirit. Reviewing a book on Irish folksongs, Wilde writes: "It is, of course, true that the highest expression of life is to be found not in the popular songs, however poetical, of any nation, but in the great masterpieces of self-conscious

Art; yet it is pleasant sometimes to leave the summit of Parnassus to look at the wild-flowers in the valley, and to turn from the lyre of Apollo to listen to the reed of Pan. We can still listen to it" (*R* 63). Wilde's allegiance is to the world and to art, but he can "still listen" to these echoes from below. In reviewing *The Feeling for Nature in Scottish Poetry*, Wilde writes that "criticism which is based on patriotism is always provincial in its result" (*R* 189–90), yet he praises the book for its delight in the poems. With similar critical aplomb, Wilde questions whether a revival of a native Irish school of architecture, however "laudable," could succeed in expressing the modern spirit: "it is not probable that the artistic genius of the Irish people will, even when 'the land has rest,' find in such interesting imitations its healthiest or best expression. Still, there are certain elements of beauty in ancient Irish art that the modern artist would do well to study" (250). The artistic genius of a country, then, is not a function simply of rootedness; its flowering, the emergence of national character in general, depends upon a certain uprootedness. Wilde actually insists in "The Critic as Artist" that "it is only by contact with the art of foreign nations that the art of a country gains that individual and separate life that we call nationality" (*I* 162).

Wilde's Irishness thus figures significantly in his cosmopolitanism: as his extraction in both senses of the term. In a review he wrote: "What captivity was to the Jews, exile has been to the Irish" (*R* 477). According to Katherine Worth, Wilde was the first of the extraordinary line of Irish-European playwrights who helped fashion a modernist European drama. ("It is wonderfully appropriate—prophetic even," writes Worth, "that *Salomé*, the play which first took up the influences from Maeterlinck and the French symbolists and projected them into a dramatic form that instantly seized the European imagination, should have been written by an Irishman living out of Ireland and writing in French—as if he were holding out his hand across fifty years to Beckett"[4]). In contrast to the exiled condition of the cosmopolitan, the nomad cannot be 'exiled' since he has no roots; his wandering is a condition of his being rather than something he has willed or chosen. The ethnic element is essential to any authentic cosmopolitanism: it is the basis of the cosmopolitan's curious, melancholy, voluntary exile.

On what then is this paradoxically detached membership in the world contingent? On art, as the reviews quoted above make clear. This is what distinguishes cosmopolitanism from the internationalism

25

of Karl Marx and Leon Trotsky; its philosophical significance must be grasped *through* art. Cosmopolitanism in European literature first arose in the work of the Swiss-born Jean-Jacques Rousseau, who in his engagement with English literature brought about a merger of Germanic and Romance strains of thought. The defining tendency of the French cosmopolitanism of the eighteenth century was to protest, in the name of modern literature, the dominance of classical models in literary works of the preceding century. Vividly expressing the cultural communism that is the essence of the cosmopolitan idea, Françoise Voltaire wrote, "we obtain kindling from our neighbors, light our own fire with it, pass it on to others, and it becomes the property of all."[5] As a literary theory, cosmopolitanism took shape and was popularized after the French Revolution in the work of Madame de Staël, whose work Wilde knew and admired.[6] The cosmopolitan strain in early European romanticism, existing together with its nationalistic tendencies, is part of the inheritance of the Enlightenment, one of those "suppressed transitions that unite all contrasts," as George Eliot puts it,[7] and it is suggested in the remarkable achievements in translation of some of the early romantics, like A. W. Schlegel, who translated Shakespeare, and Johann Heinrich Voss.[8] In turn, English romantic writers in the early years of the French Revolution were intoxicated by French influences, a spell to be broken with the turn of events in France that accompanied the rise of Napoleon. William Wordsworth lamented that the French had "become oppressors in their turn. . . . losing sight of all which they had struggled for."[9] After his disillusionment, Wordsworth renewed his link with the English countryside that had given him his greatest moments of vision, and romanticism in general would be characterized by an increasing sense of allegiance to one's native soil. Although all of the great Victorian prose writers would engage foreign literatures and philosophies, they remained self-consciously English in their use of such influences and, like Newman when he "went over to Rome," were most patriotic precisely at moments of renunciation.

Arnold's letters, particularly those written to his sister Jane, dwell on the inner war between his worldliness and his attachment to England, which he conceives of largely as a struggle between his "natural tendency" to receive European influences and his conviction of the ethical superiority of resisting them. "I am by nature so very different from you," he writes to his sister in 1851: "The worldly element enters so much more largely into my composition, that as I become *formed* there seems to grow a gulf between us. . . . But as . . . some philosophers advised to consort with our enemies because by them we were most surely apprised of our faults, so I intend not to give myself the rein in following my natural tendency, but to make war against it till it ceases to isolate me from you, and leaves me with the power to discern and adopt the good which you have, and I have not." Writing to A. H. Clough from Europe, Arnold says, "I must try how soon I can ferociously turn towards England."[10] This was in 1849. By 1867, with the publication of *Culture and Anarchy*, the divided and contradictory spirit of Arnold's nationalism would achieve its refined expression.

The rise of virulent nationalism colored the perspective of most of the Victorian prose writers who, in one way or another, were possessed by the nationalist spirit. One has only to take note of the racialist argument in *Culture and Anarchy* to see this spirit at work at the highest level.[11] Only the cultural atmosphere this created can explain how two nonconformists like George Bernard Shaw and H. G. Wells could have lent their support to the war "their" empire was waging against the Boers, rationalizing its brutalities by claiming it was in the interests of civilization.[12] Like E. M. Forster, Wilde saw the connection between British imperialism and British empiricism, and saw beyond both. If Forster located his solution to England's political and spiritual ills in the subtle chthonic nationalism of *Howards End*, with its closing animadversions against the metropolis, corporate industry, and urban culture, he affirms cosmopolitanism and the spirit of art in his half-German Schlegels. Of the three Schlegel siblings, Margaret represents a mean between the two excesses of aesthetic sensibility in Tibby and Helen: the one represents the cultivated intellect cut off from instinct and feeling, the other aesthetic feeling cut off from judgment. In Wilde's critique of the overrefinement of James Abbott Whistler's *l'art pour l'art*[13] and in his continued emphasis upon criticism, we see his effort to arrive at a similar mean. But there are of course important differences between the two writers. If for Forster art is a "signpost" to a higher spirituality, as he writes in *Howards End*, for Wilde (as for Nietzsche) art is not a signpost to something else—it *is* that something else. Wilde's "cosmopolitan criticism," as he called it, bespeaks a philosophy of ethical aestheticism that does not point elsewhere but always back to its own paradoxical truths. By definition, cosmopolitan criticism calls nationalism into question, aware of its tendency towards racism, imperialism, and war, at the same time that it recognizes "national inheritance[s]" such as art.[14]

Wilde would have been attuned to the origins of the cosmopolitan idea as inscribed in the position taken by the Stoics against the traditional distinction between Greeks and barbarians.[15] Since all people share one common reason and are subject to one divine Logos, the true Stoic sage is not a citizen of any one city but of the whole civilized world. Stoic cosmopolitanism broke with the Greek assumption of their own racial and linguistic superiority. It also helped to prepare the acceptance of early Christianity, in which, according to the Apostle Paul, there is neither Jew nor Gentile, freeman nor slave. This ancient conception of cosmopolitanism no doubt influenced Wilde, who was deeply tied to the Greeks from his youth and who, as he grew older, became increasingly engaged by earliest Christianity.

Wilde's cosmopolitan aestheticism, then, possessing as it does this long shadow, is a much weightier achievement than has been recognized by those who take the view that late nineteenth-century aestheticism is no more than an antibourgeois—that is, superlatively bourgeois—reaction against a utilitarian culture. The relatively passive state of philosophical achievement in late nineteenth-century England and France makes it that much more significant. The two dominant trends in philosophy, French positivism, associated with the school of Auguste Comte, and British empiricism, associated with Mill and Herbert Spencer, subordinated themselves to science. Even Pater's aestheticism is based on a science of "physical life," the motion of "natural elements to which science gives their names." But unlike Pater, Wilde was in sympathy as much with the classical and German philosophical tradition as with the English and French. In his early twenties he is writing in his notebook at Oxford, "It is rem. that with the rise of the philosophy of History in Greece was a feeling of cosmopolitanism chiefly among the Cynics[.] [T]he same thing occured [sic] in Germany at the time of the German Illumination in such men as Goethe, Frederick, Lessing, Fichte" (*ON* 167). Renewing Greek and German strains of thought, Wilde's critical dialogues and essays, together with the critical intelligence realized in his novel and plays, comprise an original philosophical statement. Though not as broad or momentous as that of his contemporary Nietzsche, it makes its own unique contribution to the international tradition of ideas on art, as later discussions (including a comparison to Nietzsche) show.

Wilde's contact with French literature is also important to his cosmopolitanism. From his days at Oxford, he had admired Charles Baudelaire, who in 1855 wrote of the critical importance of acquiring "the divine grace of cosmopolitanism"—a rare gift but one that *can* be acquired—which makes possible a "transformation" in the experience of foreign works of art in particular. Like the France that becomes part of Goethe's own cultivation in the discussion of cosmopolitanism in "The Critic as Artist," "a whole new world of ideas," writes Baudelaire, "is summoned in the cosmopolitan as he experiences unfamiliar art, which becomes "part and parcel of him and . . . [accompanies] him as memories till his death."[16] In *The Picture of Dorian Gray*, Wilde writes, "one had ancestors in literature, as well as in one's own race."

Wilde lived in a historical period in which the spirit of cosmopolitanism was beginning to flourish. In the last quarter of the nineteenth century, artists and writers—including Wilde, Edmund Gosse, Arthur Symons, Whistler, Stéphane Mallarmé, Paul Verlaine, Aubrey Beardsley, and Max Beerbohm—journeyed back and forth across the channel. European refugees from Germany, Italy, and France arrived after 1848 as British policy extended hospitality to political dissidents. During the same period in which Britain's "rapidly growing immigrant population raised public anxieties about cultural 'invasion,' " improved printing techniques led to the widespread dissemination of reproductions by either old masters or contemporary artists that cumulatively celebrated "Englishness."[17] The gulf between sentimental or "low" art with nationalistic subject matter and the "high" art of cosmopolitan culture widened and clarified the cultural character of the aesthetic movement. The way in which mass production threatened the "aura" of original works of art, as Walter Benjamin would later suggest, contributed to that sense of an abyss between debased public taste and the serious appreciation of particular works of art that Wilde repeatedly emphasizes. Through contact with continental culture English writers found an escape from middlebrow English taste in the last quarter of the century. Whereas Jane Austen had declined to meet Madame de Staël at the beginning of the century, Wilde was threatening to take up residence in France at the end of it, when the Lord Chamberlain banned a production of *Salomé*.

Like that of Rousseau, Wilde's intense individualism is of a piece with his cosmopolitanism. In theory, cosmopolitanism appears to surrender at the outset all possibility of accounting for anything beyond the individual, yet in practice, cosmopolitan criticism engages the spirit of nationality in understanding above all that the distinctive differences among literatures, architectures, paintings, and so on are necessarily bound up with the specific differences among peoples. (Wilde's reviews display this awareness again and again.) Could the Gothic cathedral be the work of the architects and craftsmen of any other era? Wilde learned from Ruskin that they could not, yet, breaking with Ruskin, he undertakes the responsibility to assimilate a local principle with a universal principle. The bonds of blood, native soil, speech, history, and custom are comprehended in order to be superseded. "Criticism will annihilate race-prejudice, by insisting on the unity of the human mind in the variety of its forms" (*I* 218–19).

Wilde's cosmopolitan aestheticism is not then some universalized inwardness divorced from politics, but the preliminary for a global polity; it is rooted in the advanced aestheticism of the dialogues, which is not to be confused with the earlier dandyism or with a shallow, fin-de-siècle love of the exotic. The word *exotic*, Wilde suggests, merely expresses the rage of the philistine against the unfamiliar. Cosmopolitanism suggests familiarity with things foreign and has many imposters: eclecticism, exoticism, parlor bohemianism, the will to convert, all missionary impulse, and the many forms of veiled imperialism including that grudging *toleration* that is the mental state of the disappointed missionary.[18] These are not to be confused with the cosmopolitan ideal of unaggressive, multicentered ironic *coexistence*—something similar perhaps to Kant's "unsocial sociability" (*ungesellige Geselligkeit*). "Selfishness is not living as one wishes to live, it is asking others to live as one wishes to live." The political spirit that Wilde defends in "The Soul of Man under Socialism" (which shows the influence of Mill's *On Liberty*) is at bottom a cosmopolitan spirit that "recognizes infinite variety of type as a delightful thing, accepts it, acquiesces in it, enjoys it" (*I* 328). In Leadville, Colorado, in the high Rockies, Wilde read to the miners passages from the autobiography of Benvenuto Cellini. He had supper at the bottom of a mine and recorded the "amazement of the miners when they saw art and appetite could go hand in hand" and no doubt when they also saw that Wilde could drink them under the table. That the whole American tour, as Ellmann wrote, was "an achievement in courage and grace"[19] is often forgotten in the emphasis on Wilde's self-publicity.

Irony, which in Wilde was manifest as wit, is not the ornament but the essence of cosmopolitanism. During his tour of America it often took the form of an insight rare in a colonizing epoch: awareness that savagery and refinement are universal. "Every people is academic in judging others, every people is barbaric when being judged"—so writes Baudelaire of the difficulties facing the cosmopolitan critic.[20] Wilde noted in the gun-carrying miners a refinement that came from living daily with the possibility of explosive violence, and he praised their superior manners: "There is no chance for roughness. The revolver is their book of etiquette." He took note of the mutuality of self-interest: " 'I had hoped that in their grand, simple way they would have offered me shares in "The Oscar," ' " said Wilde of a mine named in honor of his visit, " 'but in their artless untutored fashion they did not.' "[21] Wilde's witticisms have survived as the minor masterpieces they are because they express a philosophy—at once aristocratic and democratic in its bearing.

In "The Soul of Man under Socialism," Wilde would reconcile these two conflicting strains in his surprising reading of early Christianity: by emphasizing, that is, the idea of Jesus's particular individuality, or what he calls his "personality," and the demands he placed on the individual person in his life and teachings. The church and the philanthropic doctrine of the "brotherhood of man," Wilde never tired of pointing out, is morally and politically suspect and conflicts with Christ's own antinomian conduct and philosophy. In other words, anticipating the arguments of writers as diverse as Nietzsche, Friedrich Engels, and Simone Weil, Wilde distinguishes in decisive fashion between Christianity and Christendom. "The Ideals that we owe to Christ are the ideals of the man who abandons society entirely, or of the man who resists society absolutely" (*I* 331). When Jesus was told that his family wished to speak to him outside of the temple, he said, " 'Who is my mother? Who are my brothers?' . . . When one of his followers asked leave to go and bury his father, 'Let the dead bury the dead,' was his terrible answer. He would allow no claims whatsoever to be made on personality" (292). Later, in *De Profundis*, Wilde would describe Christ as one who "gave to man an extended, a Titan personality. Since his coming the history of each separate individual is, or can be made, the history of the world" (*DP* 208). Considered in their context, these statements are part of a larger exploration of individualism as a goal of *politics*, not an escape into the Palace of Art. Behind this whole line of reasoning, I would suggest, is Immanuel Kant's "Idea for a Universal History with a Cosmopolitan Intent" (1784).

It was Kant who (after Locke) shaped the philosophical and political possibilities of cosmopolitanism with his ideal of a "universal cosmopolitan nation"; such a nation is at once individualistically grounded and federally organized. To Kant, social unity can be established neither at the level of the nation or political state ("a so-called *balance of power in Europe* is a mere figment of imagination"[22]), nor in some universalized aesthetic domain separate from politics, but only by means of a "federation of peoples" or a "league" in which "every nation, even the smallest, can expect to have security and rights."[23] Kant was well aware that this ideal would be seen by leaders of nations as "pedantically childish" and "academic," "true" in theory but "useless" in practice. In his essay "On the Proverb: That May Be True in Theory, But Is of No Practical Use" (1793), he accordingly develops the point that "What on rational grounds is true in theory is also useful in practice."[24] Wilde, who studied Kant at Oxford, would in essence repeat this in his striking declaration that

> a map of the world that does not include Utopia is not worth glancing at, for it leaves out the one country at which Humanity is always landing. And when Humanity lands there, it looks out, and, seeing a better country, sets sail. Progress is the realization of Utopias. (*I* 299)
>
> For what is a practical scheme? *A practical scheme is either a scheme that is already in existence, or a scheme that could be carried out under existing conditions.* But it is exactly the existing conditions that one objects to; and any scheme that could accept these conditions is wrong and foolish. The conditions will be done away with, and human nature will change. (*I* 326)

Wilde's utopia of fulfilled individualism is to be found on a map drawn by Kant; it is the land toward which Kant's "universal cosmopolitan nation" is always moving.[25] What Wilde has in mind is a situation in which the individual himself is like a nation, secured with rights and acknowledging the rights of others. Behind Wilde's self-parody of his own self-regard (he had his hair curled to emulate the hairstyle of a Roman emperor whose bust he admired) lay a serious philosophy about the overriding importance of the individual in our conception of the world.

Again, research into Wilde's notebooks and Commonplace Book at Oxford has shown how well-versed Wilde was in philosophy and science; Georg Hegel's influence in particular has been stressed in Philip E. Smith and Michael S. Helfand's comprehensive introduction to these documents.[26] Yet Wilde writes as well, I suggest, in the worldly postrationalist spirit of Kant, whose combination of constructivism and revolutionary repeal, whose emphasis on the reality of experience, but experience informed by transcendental guidelines, he shares. When, at the conclusion of "The Critic as Artist," Wilde writes of the "true culture that is our aim" as a "perfection of those to whom sin is impossible . . . because they can do everything they wish without hurt to the soul, and can wish for nothing that can do the soul harm" (*I* 222), his writing goes back beyond Hegel's vast synthesis of morality and happiness to the critical idealism of Kant, in which the highest good is "that idea of reason in which . . . free rational beings are both totally moral and perfectly happy."[27] This idea is not a mere philosophical fantasy, but one to which we actually draw near each time we acknowledge the discrepancies between morality and happiness in the world, as Wilde's witty aphorisms repeatedly do and as he does most tragically in *De Profundis*: "To be entirely free, and at the same time entirely dominated by law is the eternal paradox of human life that we realize at every moment."

In the *Critique of Pure Reason*, Kant had shown that reason in itself could substantiate contrary positions; his presentation of the antinomies adumbrates a logic of contradiction that would only unfold in the course of the next two centuries, a logic that Wilde would pursue with refined audacity in that last offshoot of the Enlightenment, "The Decay of Lying." At once a scion of the Enlightenment and a rebel against it, Wilde questions the view held almost universally by Enlightenment thinkers that the core of humankind's advancement is increase of knowledge. Improvement of the material conditions of life is not enough; it will not necessarily reduce superstition and intolerance. Wilde regards socialism much as Kant regards knowledge: as a means to an end. Unless learning and social justice are placed in the service of appropriate ends, that is, spiritual ends, they cannot truly benefit individuals or society at large. This is so because, as Kant maintains, human beings are *ends in themselves*: "The only being which has the purpose of its existence in itself is *man*."[28] This idea traveled from Kant through Carlyle and

Pater to the young Wilde, if not directly from Wilde's reading of Kant at Oxford. It is Kant's most perilous legacy to Wilde.

To Kant, each person has a dual aspect: the self that appears to oneself as all other perceivable objects appear, and the agent who thinks—that is, who is conscious of this self in "apperception," who thinks about it and what it ought to do. The mere fact that we think is, for Kant, sufficient grounds for believing in freedom. There is an aspect of each person—the moral life—whose animating principle is free rationality, and its fundamental goal is to further the growth of this rationality by providing for it the circumstances in which to develop. This is Kant's point when he writes that man is an end in himself, and not merely a means to be arbitrarily used by this or that interest. The living self-conscious individual is arguably the logical and practical foundation of Kant's metaphysical architecture, the beginning and end of philosophizing. The parallel in Wilde may be found in the pedagogic and indeed prophetic value appertaining to the claims of individuality. In both Kant and Wilde, the individual is a social *potential* that must be cultivated for itself.

Accordingly, Kant argues that humanity consider its development as one of nature's objectives. Ted Humphrey writes that

> The human characteristic serving as the means through which humanity's capacities come to be refined is 'antagonism,' which Kant also calls 'unsocial sociability.' . . . This characteristic permeates all levels of human relations, beginning with those among single individuals and extending to those among nations. All individuals—be they persons, families, peoples, or nations—have needs that cannot by themselves be adequately met; this forces them to seek out relations with other individuals. . . . [In the end] real accommodations of other parties is necessary. Such accommodations takes the form of recognizing that all parties involved have rights that accrue to them just because they, like oneself, are ends in themselves, who cannot rightfully be used as means to one's own ends, i.e. takes the form of acknowledging them to be persons.[29]

On a macroscale this translates to Kant's federalist ideal; on a microscale it corresponds to Wilde's emphasis on individual development, wherein utopianism is necessarily tempered by irony, by a realistic grasp of human nature and human antagonism. Is not "unsocial sociability" a suitable formula for the world of his plays and his novel, for his relations to Douglas, and for his understanding of the cosmopolitan ideal?

The distinct place occupied by the aesthetic in Kant, its theoretic separation from the other faculties, would provide the basis for all aestheticism to follow, but among the great aesthetes at the beginning of the modern period (Baudelaire, Nietzsche, and Wilde) it was Wilde who would remain closest to Kant's rational ideal of self-development. In "An Answer to the Question: What Is Enlightenment?" (1784) Kant had written, "*Enlightenment is man's emergence from his self-imposed immaturity. Immaturity* is the inability to use one's understanding without guidance from another."[30] Half of society (the female half) is kept like "domestic livestock," Kant observes, afraid to take the step to maturity and think for themselves. Wilde writes, "A man who does not think for himself does not think at all" (*I* 328). "All imitation in morals and in life is wrong" (293), if one is to develop. "Whatever is realised is right," he concludes in *De Profundis*. Claiming to go beyond conventions in morality (as he in fact went beyond them), Wilde's aphorisms nonetheless retain a decidedly moral inflection ("is wrong," "is right"); he does not transvalue these predicates in quite the way Nietzsche will do, but remains closer to both Kant and the Victorians in his faith in human development. Nevertheless, Wilde subtly turns the vocabulary of English moral and social criticism against itself, allowing its latent contradictions to emerge; and, in so doing, he brings about a transformation from within.

Wilde's Debt to the Victorians

One of Wilde's heroes (and a decisive precedent) wrote in 1855 that

> Like all my friends I have tried to lock myself into a system, so as to be able to pontificate as I liked. But a system is a kind of damnation that condemns us to perpetual backsliding; we are always having to invent another. . . . And every time, my system was beautiful, big, spacious, convenient, tidy and polished above all; at least so it seemed to me. And every time, some spontaneous unexpected product of universal vitality would come and give the lie to my puerile and old-fashioned wisdom. . . . Under the threat of being constantly humiliated by another conversion, I took a big decision. To escape from the horror of these philosophic apostasies, I arrogantly resigned myself to modesty; I became content to feel; I came back and sought sanctuary in impeccable naïveté . . . and at least I can now declare, in so far as a man can answer for his virtues, that my mind now enjoys a more abundant impartiality.

Baudelaire then proclaims that only in this flexible state of mind will expressions of beauty thrive: "in the manifold productions of art, there is something always new, something that will eternally escape from the rules and the analyses of the school!"[31]

Like Baudelaire, Wilde sought sanctuary in the "impeccable naiveté" and "abundant impartiality" of cosmopolitanism, because the different systems left him by the Victorians failed *as systems*, individually and collectively, even though they succeeded in providing him with an abundant storehouse of ideas. In Wilde (as in Baudelaire), such impartiality is not to be confused with a passive eclecticism.[32] Wilde actively gathers and juxtaposes the contradictory ideas among the Victorians, removing them from context in order to generate certain philosophical possibilities or hypotheses. He cites opposing notions—for example, Mill's ethical idea of liberty and Arnold's aesthetic idea of culture—when he sums up the argument of "The Soul of Man under Socialism" with the statement that "The new Individualism is the new Hellenism" (*I* 335). Ruskin's Christian theology of art is likewise conjoined to Pater's Pagan theology of experience through much of Wilde's later work. "And exactly as in Art," he writes in a section of *De Profundis* that leads to a meditation on the figure of Jesus, "one is only concerned with what a particular thing is at a particular moment to oneself, so it is also in the ethical evolution of one's character" (197). In the review of the Victorians that follows, we shall see that these far-reaching hypotheses, based on citations that transform their respective contexts, were made necessary by the incapacity of the individual systems themselves to integrate both ethical and aesthetic experience. The blood and bones of Wilde's cosmopolitan radicalism—a radicalism normally associated with France—developed from his engagement with the Victorians.[33]

In Carlyle's "Signs of the Times" (1829), we see one of the earliest and most pronounced articulations of the theoretic deadlock that would characterize the discourse of the major prose writers of the century. In Carlyle, it appears as a conflict between the "dynamic" and the "mechanical." In Mill, it would be understood as an opposition between inner, emotional and aesthetic needs and outer, ethical and political responsibilities. In Arnold, it becomes Hellenism (spontaneity of consciousness) versus Hebraism (strictness of conscience). Here, the differing formulations of these writers, all of them grounded in a framework of antithesis, are subsumed under the categorical opposition of the ethical and the aesthetic. (A characteristic of nineteenth-century thought in general, this opposition finds one of its greatest expressions, as I indicate at the end of chapter 1, outside of England in Kierkegaard's *Either/Or* [1843].) At times the ethical side of this opposition (for example, Arnold's Hebraism) is conceived in terms that we associate with liberalism; at other times (in Mill, for instance) it is associated with a moral conservatism that borders on social repression. In some writers, as in Arnold, the ethical is intimately tied up with the religious, whereas in others, like Carlyle, it is understood more as a secular impulse to organize society. The notion of a uniform Victorian ethical ideal must accordingly be resisted. On the other hand, though its political associations fluctuate sharply, as Terry Eagleton has shown in *Ideology of the Aesthetic*,[34] the meaning of the word *aesthetic* (concerned with perception, beauty, spontaneity, inwardness) remains fairly constant in these writers. What interests me for the present, however, is the opposition itself.

In "Signs of the Times," Carlyle characterizes this opposition in terms of a threat to the "dynamic" spirit of life, particularly to the dynamism of the inner life. Not only has the mechanical ideal of adapting means to ends infiltrated every walk of life and all institutions from the educational to the juridical, but a crisis is taking place in the form of what Carlyle identifies as a mechanization of the inner life. Carlyle's example is the degradation of religious life; no longer based on wonder or revelation, religious experience has become at bottom "a wise prudential feeling grounded on mere calculation . . . whereby some smaller quantum of earthly enjoyment may be exchanged for a larger quantum of celestial enjoyment."[35] As one whose whole conception of inwardness is essentially religious, Carlyle does not investigate the more secular manifestations of his idea of inner mechanization in the way, for example, his contemporary Jane Austen does in her novels. In *Emma* the heroine's entire inner being is absorbed in planning and strategy, in "adapting means to ends," in a way that threatens to bring about only inner waste, something comically redeemed at the end of *Emma* but more painfully exposed in Austen's last novel, *Persuasion*. There the estranged heroine's slow reconciliation with her lover is repeatedly thwarted by minor circumstantial or mechanical obstacles as the novel draws to a close, setting off a silent intimacy between the two characters that is expressed in ever more frequent allusions to eyes and hands. This unspoken, spontaneous intimacy or shared inwardness is endangered in the formally prearranged, moribund social world of *Persuasion*. The eruption of intimacy that takes place a century later in the novels of D. H. Lawrence, who was in many ways a spiritual scion of Carlyle, is rooted in the same impulse that made Wilde "live in the enjoyment of his own spontaneity,"[36] to use Yeats's phrase. Carlyle laments the loss of spontaneous religious feeling; Arnold, in less passionate but grander tones, complains of the undervaluing of "spontaneity of consciousness" in the lives of Englishmen. But Wilde had the courage of *their* convictions and would put these ideas into practice in the most intimate way by attempting to live his very life as a work of art, that is, refusing to adapt means to ends but being, in the most resonant way possible, open to reading each particular concern at the particular moment of its recognition. At the end of his life, in *De Profundis*, he would invoke for this profoundly improvisatory orientation an ethical-aesthetic temporality: "exactly as in Art one is only concerned with what a particular thing is at a particular moment to oneself, so it is also in the ethical evolution of one's character."

The intellectual groundwork for this philosophic correlation of ethics and aesthetics dates back to Wilde's years at Oxford. In the *Oxford Notebooks* he alludes to Baudelaire, who earlier had hinted at the closeness of the "dandy" and the "moralist." (In his "Journals and Notebook," Baudelaire writes of "the necessity of leading an intensely moral life: an exemplary life—lived, so to speak, in front of a mirror."[37] In "My Heart Laid Bare" he insists that the Dandy "should live and sleep in front of a mirror"[38]). As the *Notebooks* clearly show, however, the idiom by which Wilde, in his youth, conceptualized the relations between ethics and aesthetics derives from a German-influenced English philosophical prose. He writes in his Commonplace Book—note the analytically colored choice of words— that "to treat life in the spirit of art is to treat it as a thing in which means and end are identified. . . . To withdraw the thoughts from the machinery of life to fix them with appropriate emotions on the great facts of human life wh[ich] machinery does not affect [.] . . . The end of life must be realised through the means" (*ON* 141–42). In these lines Wilde reveals his debt to Carlyle and to Kant as much as to Pater.[39] In "Conceptions of the Self in an Age of Progress," Steven Marcus directs our attention to the polarity between Carlyle's emphasis on work, on dedication to a value outside of oneself, and Wilde's emphasis on the self (as a work of art). In reference to Wilde's remark to Gide that he had put his genius into his life and only his talent into his work, Marcus comments: "We have arrived at a point at which Carlyle has been stood on his head."[40] But it was really Carlyle who himself had prepared this development. In Wilde we see not the negation but the fulfillment of Carlyle's spiritual analysis of the times.

In "Signs of the Times," for example, Carlyle writes that "Freedom, without which indeed all spiritual life is impossible, depends on infinitely more complex influences than either the extension or the curtailment of the 'democratic interest,' " and he argues that changes in government institutions, while they may be "much . . . are not all."[41] Similarly, Wilde would later argue that socialism cannot realize its goals, which have everything to do with a perfected spiritual life, until individuals achieve harmony within themselves and with their environment. Wilde dismissed Carlyle's later authoritarianism, while developing his predecessor's original analysis of the soul of man under English capitalism into the achieved political statement, "The Soul of Man under Socialism."

Wilde would make a similarly inventive and liberating use of the life and work of John Henry Cardinal Newman, the Anglican minister who converted to Catholicism in 1845. The influence is not to be found, as some have thought, in Wilde's interest in Catholicism. Although Wilde was preoccupied with the figure of Jesus from his early years, his perennial toying with formal conversion to Catholicism had the air of insolence from beginning to end.[42] Newman's influence on Wilde may be seen, first, in the forward-moving, incisive energy of a prose that maintains its momentum despite the witty insinuations and digressions. If Carlyle's prose, in its biblical reminiscences, gathers in and shores up various spiritual charges, rendered small explosions by the capitals, then the language of Newman's *Apologia Pro Vita Sua* gives an impression of the *shedding* of garments, namely, a past theology or ideology, and a moving forward toward the fully naked intellectual and spiritual position that will prepare his conversion. Suspense is generated by the reiteration of arguments against Catholicism that are finally overcome. Wilde's two dialogues on art operate in a similar manner. The main speaker in each is always moving toward the most extreme affirmation of the theology of art, toward absolute conversion, as it were, his fervor both checked and increased by the resistance of his listener. But Wilde's speaker, unlike Newman's "converted" narrative voice, never arrives at a full conversion; the dialogue form itself prevents that.[43] Unlike Newman, Wilde is forever skating on thin ice, much like Newman before his conversion in the *Apologia*, but never arriving at the moment of conversion: "Supposing I were crossing ice . . . which I had good reasons for considering sound . . . and supposing a stranger from the bank, in a voice of authority, and in an earnest tone, warned me that it was dangerous, and then was silent, I think I should be startled, and should look about me anxiously, but I think too that I should go on, till I had better grounds for doubt."[44] Certain of the existence of an immaterial, ethical ideal in the being of God, and equally certain of the reality of misery in the world that his senses communicated to him (what he calls "the sight of the world"), Newman comes to the conclusion that only the Roman Catholic Church, an institutional "power" introduced into the world by the creator, can maintain truth amidst the anarchy of the senses. The opposition between ethics and *aesthesis* is then overcome for Newman by means of a commitment to something conceived to be external to himself: the rituals of the Roman Catholic Church. In his own words, the conversion represented an absolute security, like "coming into port after a rough sea." The more Protestant Wilde denied himself the sense of security that comes of locking oneself into a system, as Baudelaire phrases it, and remained true to the provisional character of experience by accepting the inner uncertainty that comes with *living* in a condition of aesthetic and ethical experiment. Ethics could not be decided for him by an act of allegiance to some fixed authority, but was something within the person that continues to evolve by means of aesthetic perception and analogical reasoning.

In a century of almost programmatic spiritual crisis and overcoming, Newman's experience and its literary harvest had a subtle influence on Wilde. The shadow of Newman was still felt at Oxford when Wilde was there, and he praises the *Apologia* in the opening pages of "The Critic as Artist." *De Profundis* is a kind of heretical *Apologia*, falling within the Protestant tradition of inward risk that begins with another work written in prison, John Bunyan's *Pilgrim's Progress*. In Wilde's view, the *Apologia* was also brought to birth in a kind of prison: "the world will never weary of watching that troubled soul in its progress from darkness to darkness," he writes drily of Newman (*I* 101). But the model of inward risk stayed with him: a model of inner development toward a sublime overcoming of the opposition between the ethical and the aesthetic, rather than an embattled declaration of the opposition, such as Carlyle provides.

Furthermore, Newman's decision to "go over to Rome" is imagined, as the phrase itself suggests, in terms of a departure from England, a breaking of the most sentimental national attachments to his parish and college for the sake of a new theology. Wilde too would transcend nationality and embrace a theology of art, one that, like Catholicism, had its own love of costume and decoration, and its own cosmopolitanism.

The theology of art itself, at least in its English-language provenance, was rooted in the work of Wilde's teacher, Ruskin, and later, in the doctrines of the Pre-Raphaelites. Like Newman, Ruskin attempted to overcome the ethical-aesthetic duality by means of Christian doctrine, arguing that in the Christian art of the Middle Ages we find the perfect expression of ethical truth: the savage, changeable, natural imperfection of human life opposed to the immutable perfection of God. This is why "Taste . . . is the ONLY morality," as Ruskin says in "Traffic"[45]—that is, the only morality is to be found in a Christian aesthetic of "taste." Ruskin finds the Egyptian pyramid ugly for ethical reasons: a slave economy is apparent in its very form.

Wilde's engagement with Greek art and literature alone would make Ruskin's Christian synthesis of the ethical and the aesthetic seem too narrow, and his reviews from a young age evince his cosmopolitan sensibility. (Included among reviews of over two hundred books are discussions of Chuang-tzu, Madame de Staël, Walt Whitman, Honoré de Balzac, George Sand, Fyodor Dostoyevsky, and of course studies and translations of Greek literature.) For this reason, Wilde would presumably have noted the equivocal character of Ruskin's ideals, something that Proust was actually the first to describe: "The doctrines he professed were moral and not aesthetic doctrines, and yet he chose them for their beauty. And since he did not wish to present them as beautiful but as true, he was forced to deceive himself about the nature of the reasons that made him adopt them. Hence there was such a continual compromising of conscience."[46] Proust accuses Ruskin of "idolatry," a charge that is in some sense borne out by the full-blown idolatry of Ruskin's followers, the Pre-Raphaelites.

As Wilde's critical genius unfolds, we find repeated references to Ruskin's critical ideas, particularly in "The Soul of Man under Socialism." There Wilde would argue that art as we know it reflects the worship of pain that is inevitable in an unjust Christian society. (It may do this by artificial reaction against the ugliness and pain of life as much as by more obvious tragic or melodramatic representations.) Ruskin's beloved Gothic, with its savagery, contortion, and "mental disturbance," would be the prime example of such art; in Wilde's view it is the quintessential Christian art because "the medieval Christ is the real Christ," one who realized his perfection through pain, and who made no direct attempt to reconstruct society. If society is reformed in a sufficiently large-spirited manner, however, art would become more beautiful because it would no longer reflect the worship of pain.

In "The Soul of Man under Socialism," as in "The Decay of Lying," Wilde therefore calls upon art to distance itself, therapeutically as it were, from modern life and society—not to imitate them, but to uplift and stimulate them with new forms of expression. Because "Life is Art's best, Art's only pupil" (*I* 34), artists have a pedagogic responsibility to "Life" not to descend to the level of the student. In contrast, the mature Ruskin of *Unto This Last* would call upon the political economists to reform their morals in the hopes of bettering society. In Wilde's view, such hopes for reformation were as futile as the Hinksey Road experiment. The imagination of the political economist must be radically altered before ethical reform is possible, and such change is wrought by art, not by the sermon. Ruskin's moral idealism is emotional in temper: and that, according to Wilde, is the limitation of English ideals in general. From the point of view of Wilde's ethical aesthetic, there is perhaps no more subtle proof of the weakness of Ruskin's later critical perspective than the atrophy of his aesthetic sense, revealed in his lavish praise of the nostalgic illustrations of Kate Greenaway. It was in these idyllic pictures of small children frolicking that Ruskin's emotional and ethical vision of a better society finally came to rest.

The strain of weakness in Ruskin's thought becomes especially apparent, as I have suggested, in his followers, the Pre-Raphaelites, who may be said to represent the full development of what Proust

called Ruskin's "idolatry." Far more acquiescent in their use of
Ruskin than Wilde, the Pre-Raphaelites aesthetized Ruskin's social
criticism to an extreme, insisting on the necessity of "beauty" in
every quarter of life: in homes, furniture, clothing, and factories.
The moral and physical ugliness of industrial life justified conscious
escapism. Sir Edward Burne-Jones would say that the more his
society produced locomotives, the more he would paint pictures of
angels, revealing an attitude of self-willed blindness that may account for the soullessness of many of his paintings.[47] Early on,
Wilde expressed reservations about the Pre-Raphaelite cult of
beauty, suggesting that the power of the artist to find beauty amidst
the ugliness of modern life does not by any means solve the question of the role of beauty in *life*, however useful a reminder it may
be to the artist to stick to his craft.[48] When viewed beside the
Baudelairean ironies of "The Decay of Lying," at any rate, the Pre-
Raphaelite effort to close the gap between the moral and the aesthetic resembles wish-fulfilment, a far cry from the deeply meditated ironic utopianism of Wilde's essay on the spiritual limitations
of socialism, not to mention the heroic struggle of *De Profundis* to
comprehend aesthetically the moral shipwreck of his life.[49]

In *De Profundis*, the work in which Wilde confronts the reality
of suffering most directly, he cites Ruskin once again in a passage
that elevates medieval art over Renaissance art. His point is not to
argue for a return to a medieval ideal of life, however, as Ruskin had
done in promoting handmade crafts over industrial products, but to
stress the need for a modern development of the romantic spirit of
the Middle Ages, which the Renaissance had impeded with its attention to "dead rules." Wilde sees such a development embodied
in Baudelaire's *Fleurs du Mal* and in the Russian novel.[50] Proust's
own love of Ruskin suggests Wilde was right when he saw at last the
modernist potential of Ruskinian Gothic; at the end of his life,
Wilde's taste did not fail him, because, unlike the late Ruskin, he
never turned away from art criticism to social criticism, but maintained their vital connection.

Although for publicity purposes Wilde spoke in a Pre-
Raphaelite idiom early in his career, particularly in his lectures in
America on "the House Beautiful," it may have been the public reception of the Pre-Raphaelites, rather than their ideas, that immediately conditioned his early and continued insistence on the need
for a "higher ethics," such that only a refined aesthetic sense makes

possible. From attacks on Sir John Millais's painting in the 1850s to Robert Buchanan's famous personal assault on Dante Gabriel Rossetti in "The Fleshly School of Poetry" in 1870, the philistine campaign against "immoral" innovations in the arts maintained a decisive influence on British public opinion. Buchanan's diatribe, which included accusations of sickness and insanity, contributed to Rossetti's nervous collapse in 1872. Wilde's lengthy attacks on public taste in "The Soul of Man under Socialism" and "The Critic as Artist," influenced as they are by Rossetti's own "The Stealthy School of Criticism" and Algeron Charles Swinburne's "Notes on Poems and Ballads," may be seen as part of a reaction against the rather sadistic philistinism of his day. From Wilde's perspective, the "uncouth morals"[51] and the "sordid terror" of "middleclass respectability" prevented more than anything else the public's rising above "the vulgar standard of goodness" (*I* 221). Wilde's philosophical emphasis upon the importance of a receptive *temperament* for receiving and judging art, rather than a set of puritanical prescriptions of right and wrong, arose within an originally brutal context.

The prevailing dislike of sensuality in art expressed itself in a variety of ways, from Buchanan's horror of the flesh, in his review of Rossetti, to Arnold's dissociating the "obvious faults of our animality" from the world of "sweetness and light" in *Culture and Anarchy*. As an artist, Wilde was not concerned with depicting sensual experience itself as much as its aesthetic nuances, and so the censorious atmosphere did not particularly inhibit him. As a critic, however, he was sufficiently offended by it to go to the satiric extreme of insisting on the immorality of art. "Pen, Pencil, and Poison," Wilde's essay on the criminal and artist Thomas Griffiths Wainewright, in part parodies "pseudo-ethical criticism."[52] This was Wilde's term for the moralistic treatment of the artist's life and work found in countless journals of the period that insisted on the virtue of its subject, specifically, the edification to be derived from exposure to the artist's writing and knowledge of his or her life.[53] Wilde urges his reader to be reasonable by recognizing that "The fact of a [man's] being a poisoner is nothing against his prose" (*I* 93). In this highly amusing essay, the commonplace formula by which the artist's aesthetic sense compels him to create morally elevating works of art is reversed: Wainewright, with his fine draftsman's eye, poisons his sister-in-law partly because, it seems, he is repelled by the thickness of her ankles. As Wilde writes elsewhere, "There is nothing sane about the worship of beauty" (*I* 196).

In objecting to Victorian censorship of sensual experience in works of art, Wilde never takes the conventional liberal position in favor of freedom of expression. He knew well the writings of the leading exponent of more liberal expression in the civil sphere, John Stuart Mill, and alludes to the limitations of this point of view. The subtitle of part 2 of "The Critic as Artist"— which reads, "with some remarks upon the importance of discussing everything"—is Wilde's ironic allusion to his own exploitation of Mill.[54] For what is contained in the dialogue is not the sort of subject Mill might have championed in the well-known "freedom of discussion" passage in *On Liberty* but an erudite discourse of the sort that the newspaper-reading public could not bear.[55] Wilde must have seen the fundamental contradiction in Mill's analysis of the age's ills, particularly as it bore upon the life of the exceptional person or genius. For Mill's liberal society is based on public education, on open discussion and debate among educated, reasoning people, yet the genius, as he acknowledges, is not simply a product of such ratiocination; genius emerges and unfolds as a tree sprouts and ramifies, Mill writes. How then can genius flourish—something which Mill sees as absolutely necessary to the fruition of democracy—if the best that society can offer him is an environment of rational discussion? If the growth of genius is not a rational process, then Mill's rationalistic liberal society may be even more hostile to it than the present "irrational" one, in which free discussion is generally suppressed.

It is in this questionable opposition in *On Liberty* between the needs of the innately spontaneous "genius" and those of the much vaster population of ordinary people, who supposedly require a more conventional ethical and social order, that Mill's confirmation of the Victorian opposition between the aesthetic and the ethical is most obvious. But in the *Autobiography* as well, Mill's philosophy once again founders on this opposition. There the irresolvable contradictions arise in the context of his treatment of "happiness," specifically his own happiness and sense of fulfillment. Despite Mill's well-known and self-serving show of modesty—he insisted that he achieved what he did only because the education he received from his father put him "twenty-five years ahead of his contemporaries"—we may assume that he saw in the youthful self of his "mental crisis" an example of "genius" oppressed by its surroundings, stifled inwardly.

Though making happiness his goal in life had in fact made him miserable—the orderly, mechanical prosecution of the utilitarian goal of reforming society led to a deterioration of his inner life, what Carlyle would have called the "dynamical" side of his nature—Mill refused to abandon the goal of happiness even after his crisis. "I never, indeed, wavered in the conviction that happiness is the test of all rules of conduct, and the end of life. But I now thought that this end was only to be attained by not making it a direct end."[56] The fact is it had never been a direct end but was centered from the beginning on the admittedly unrealizable goal of reforming the world: "I was accustomed to felicitate myself on the certainty of a happy life which I enjoyed, through placing my happiness in something . . . in which some progress might be always making, while it could never be exhausted by complete attainment."[57] Here Mill refuses to accept what his entire "mental crisis" had effectively communicated to him: that happiness is an inward condition and therefore reachable not through action in the practical sphere but through cultivation of the right state of mind, something made possible by exposure to beauty or art. In the *Autobiography*, it is art that initially brings him out of his depression—specifically, a passage from Jean-François Marmontel's *Mémoires* that gives form to his emotions about his father—an example of what Wilde means when he writes that "form" is "the death of pain" (*I* 208). As in *On Liberty*, Mill acknowledges the hidden, irrational needs of human beings—specifically the needs of an exceptional person like himself—and he also would like to create a society that is more accommodating of these needs, but the society he envisions is based entirely on a rather traditional notion of reason. Designating a "private" realm to be protected by law and eventually by custom, in which greater freedom of expression is permitted, will not answer if all experience is understood in terms of utility and logical process. In the society Wilde hoped to see come into being, the "genius" would have a better chance of flourishing, according to the unacknowledged logic of Mill's own narrative. Using the word "artist" instead of genius, Wilde wrote in an early review, "An artist is not an isolated fact; he is the resultant of a certain *milieu* and a certain *entourage*, and can no more be born of a nation that is devoid of any sense of beauty than a fig can grow from a thorn or a rose blossom from a thistle" (*M* 65–66).

In "The Soul of Man under Socialism," however, Wilde does not confine his working definition of the individual to the exceptional person, "genius," or even to the artist: "I am not talking of the great imaginatively realized Individualism of such poets as I have mentioned, but of the great actual Individualism latent and potential in mankind generally" (*I* 283).[58] The "individual" is a *potential*, latent in all human beings, which cannot be realized unless the separation of public authority and private liberty is overcome, rather than reinforced, however humanely, as it is in Mill. The soul of man can unfold like a flower only after the state has achieved and moved beyond the condition of socialism, with its materialist ideals and authoritarian tendencies, to a recognition that it exists only to cultivate the individual, not to exercise authority over it; then and only then "human nature will change" (326). Whereas Mill, the pragmatist, is mainly interested in protecting those with exceptional natures against the power of public authority and opinion, Wilde, the idealist, is interested in changing both nature and our conception of it.[59] Changing the institutions of government will not change human nature, will not allow it to develop its joyous potential, until the state recognizes its own essentially provisional character, its intrinsic lack of authority in the question of *what man is*.

Wilde's argument is simply that the generality of mankind will not ultimately flower under the socialist ideal, even though socialism aims to foster the general good, because the good of humanity is not by definition general and material but individual and spiritual.[60] Socialism is a necessary stage in human development because it will eradicate poverty and the multitude of spiritual sins that come with it, not the least of which is the Victorian philanthropic identification with pain, but it is *only* a stage. Wilde both accepts and rejects socialism, just as one could say that he accepts and rejects Mill. He moves with extraordinary deftness through the Millian argument, laying waste its self-righteous utilitarianism, scrutinizing its sense of justice, and purifying its idea of liberty.

The thinker with whom Wilde is most at odds and also perhaps most deeply allied is Matthew Arnold.[61] In Arnold, the opposition between the ethical and the aesthetic receives its most mature exposition, for the upshot of Arnold's social analysis in *Culture and Anarchy* is the justification of coercion by "culture." According to Arnold, the English lack an idea of the *state*. The French possess such an idea—and why? Not because of their great philosophical and political tradition but because of French conscription. Though "culture" gives us the idea of the state, in France the military disseminates it. This insight, put forth in chapter 2 of *Culture and Anarchy*, leads subtly to the idea in the conclusion: "for resisting anarchy the lovers of culture may prize and employ fire and strength."[62]

Though the meaning of "sweetness and light" is fully stated in *Culture and Anarchy*, the meaning of its opposing image, "fire and strength" is not. "Sweetness and light" is Arnold's metaphor for culture, or the best that has been thought and said; "sweetness" is beauty, or the pleasure in beauty, pleasure without desire, such as may be found in art. (This pleasure is wholly distinct from "the obvious faults of our animality," faults or defects which Arnold sees religion as undertaking to correct.) "Light" in Arnold is intelligence or truth, a traditional, "Hellenistic" association. As a metaphorical complement to "sweetness and light," "strength" refers to religious strictness of conscience, to Hebraistic single-minded conviction, but, in spite and perhaps because of its diverse Hellenic and Christian associations, it is not entirely clear what "fire" refers to: courage? inspiration? love of freedom? All of these things, perhaps. At any rate, Arnold places this power in the service of conscience because what "fire and strength" generally represent is the Protestant English conscience and spirit of freedom. (Later, both Freud and Nietzsche would suggest that conscience is an aggressive instinct turned inward toward the self.)

In Arnold we see how disabling the Victorian opposition between ethics and aesthetics has become to art, because, according to these Arnoldian categories, culture or art in its essence lacks strength and fire. Beauty is without strength and truth without fire. No one need fear mere "culture" according to this definition. Yet the profound equivocations lurking in these unacknowledged metaphors cause Arnold's philosophy to founder. The whole point of his idea of culture or of an aesthetic ideal of community—so badly needed, he says, in England today—is that full play be given to a "disinterested curiosity," something that cannot be forced. Yet the state is ultimately a coercive apparatus in Arnold. Whenever anarchy manifests itself, "the lovers of culture" may be pressed (like Plato's guardians) to make use of "fire and strength," that is, to bring about the rapid suppression of those whose speech or actions appear to destabilize the populace. Arnold's support of his father's opinion on how to deal with rioters would suggest that the population does indeed have something to fear from "culture": "we can never forsake" his father's opinion, he writes, which was to "flog the rank and file, and fling the ring-leaders from the Tarpeian Rock!"[63] The vagueness of the metaphor of "fire" serves an important function here because, whatever fire is supposed to mean, there is no question that fire is to be feared.

In Pater's work this vaguely dangerous power would be *openly* arrogated to culture, though in a way Arnold would not have anticipated. The famous conclusion to *The Renaissance* fastens on Arnold's metaphor in a decisive fashion: "To burn always with this hard, gemlike flame, to maintain this ecstasy, is success in life."[64] It is precisely culture or art that inflames the senses; the connection, repudiated by so many Victorians from Buchanan to Arnold, has finally been made. Accordingly, in Wilde's essays, dialogues, and novels, culture, or the love of beauty, is fundamentally dangerous in its contagion—it is nothing if not the manifestation of a kind of spiritual fire—and Wilde repeatedly warns us of this salutary danger.

In much of the standard criticism on Wilde, Pater's influence has been exaggerated to the point of excluding the influences of the other Victorians discussed here.[65] Yet Pater himself designated Wilde as Arnold's true successor; he praised *Intentions* for carrying on, "more perhaps than any other writer, the brilliant critical work of Matthew Arnold." Like Arnold, Wilde understood the importance of viewing culture as a whole, as an integral rather than an aggregate. Such an integral and manifold entity must be *judged as a whole from without*—not simply from within or from the point of view of single individuals inhabiting it, as Mill tends to judge it. Without this paradoxical possibility of standing—in however linguistically conditioned a way—outside (one's own) culture, cosmopolitanism is impossible. But what, exactly, did Wilde extract from Arnold? Of the four metaphors, *sweetness*, *light*, *fire*, and *strength*, he would make particular use of the idea of *sweetness*, of love of beauty for its own sake. *Light* would remain with Arnold, for Wilde was too well-versed in the contrarieties of Victorian culture—he was too modern, which is to say, in touch with the archaic—to accept an idea of truth or intelligence as *light*. He had come to assume and indeed to exemplify an idea of truth as contradiction; light and darkness could only be understood together: "For in art there is no such thing as universal truth. A truth in art is that whose contradictory is true. And just as it is only in art-criticism, and through it, that we can apprehend the Platonic theory of ideas, so it is only in art-criticism, and through it, that we can realize Hegel's system of contraries. The truths of metaphysics are the truths of masks" (*I* 269–70). As for *strength*, Arnold's narrow rigor of conscience, Wilde could no more identify this with beauty or art than Arnold could: "I have always *wished* to believe that the line of strength and the line of beauty are one."[66] Moreover, the power of public taste in his century had led him to distrust any notion of a collective conscience and to feel the fragility of art. This left only one possibility by which to overcome the opposition between ethics and aesthetics that Arnold had finalized for his century, and here is where the influence of Pater would assert itself so decisively, making Wilde feel to the very end of his life that Pater's influence had been crucial. For Wilde would conjoin sweetness to fire. In proposing that the sense of beauty, by its power of contagion, unites human beings, Wilde took from both Pater and Arnold. Hence the cosmopolitan ideal: that it is art alone, and not "emotions" or abstract systems of ethics, that can create "a common intellectual atmosphere between all countries" (*M* 269).

In cosmopolitan criticism, or in this complex method of citing the Victorians, Wilde discovered a power that others of his age, like Baudelaire and Nietzsche, also proclaimed. In the words of their true successor, Walter Benjamin, it was "the power not to preserve but to purify, to tear from context, to destroy; the only power in which hope still resides that something might survive this age—because it was wrenched from it."[67]

3

⑤ Wilde's Reassociation of Sensibility

> Art is not something which you can take or leave.
> It is a necessity of human life.
>
> —Oscar Wilde, *Miscellanies*

An Ethical Aesthetic

It is possible to speak of Wilde's "ethical aesthetic" because Wilde was convinced that the experience of art is the only viable means in the contemporary world of countering the commercial spirit, or of arriving at that critical understanding of the past and present that is essential to a safe future. Yet Wilde did not arrive at this position through experience of art alone. At Oxford, he discovered for himself the limitations of pure metaphysics and of evolutionary science, and he applied their terms together to the concrete realms of art and life. For Wilde, art is the sensuous embodiment of spirit, the product of imagination, which itself "is the result of heredity. It is simply concentrated race experience." One cannot therefore erect social machinery around art without distorting its ideal and evolutionary character; nor can one "teach" it exactly, or institute it, that is, make it the official center of cultural authority, as Arnold had urged, for its benefits are transmitted too subtly and "atmospherically." Yet, from Wilde's point of view, any society that ignores or devalues art, or fails to see its utopian character, is basically without hope.

Wilde achieved, if you will, a "reassociation of sensibility"[1] at the end of his century when he effectively overcame the strict Victorian opposition between the ethical and the aesthetic as described in the last chapter. He did this, not by synthesizing the two, but by demonstrating their interrelatedness while still preserving a distinction between them. In part 2 of "The Critic as Artist" Wilde attempts for the first time to make the interrelation explicit. There he begins with what appears to be a contradiction of the sort found in "The Decay of Lying," which radically separates art and life at the same time that it stresses the importance of an art *of* life — that is to say, the ideal of human perfectibility:

> *Gilbert.* For Life is terribly deficient in form. Its catastrophes happen in the wrong way to the wrong people. There is a grotesque horror about its comedies, and its tragedies seem to culminate in farce. One is always wounded when one approaches it. Things last either too long, or not long enough. . . .
>
> *Ernest.* Life then is a failure?
>
> *Gilbert.* From the artistic point of view, certainly. . . . Life! Life! Don't let us go to life for our fulfillment or our experience. It is a thing narrowed by circumstances, incoherent in its utterance, and without that fine correspondence of form and spirit which is the only thing that can satisfy the artistic and critical temperament. . . .
>
> *Ernest.* Must we go, then, to Art for everything?
>
> *Gilbert.* For everything. . . . It is through Art, and through Art only, that we can realise our perfection; through Art, and through Art only, that we can shield ourselves from the sordid perils of actual existence. (*I* 164–66, 173–74)

The power of art to transform and to spiritualize us ("realise our perfection") is contingent on art's initial separation from our customary being. It is only by standing over life, as it were, it is only through maintaining distance on its sordid perils, that Art can affect human consciousness at all. Wilde is evidently attempting to have it both ways, as the subject matter itself demands, yet he skims over the uncertain claim that both art and our ability to perfect ourselves are separate from "actual existence." Wilde's method here is as usual to make fleet moves, taking up—without necessarily dwelling on—all sides of the issue, and he uses the dialogue form to manifest as elaborately as possible the problem of the separation-yet-connection of art and life.[2] (To tell the truth about an interrelation necessitates exposing any material lack of relation.) This mercurial method of composition, shifting precipitously between abstract and concrete, can always of course disguise a certain confusion of outlook. On the other hand, given Wilde's particular temperament and his peculiar notion of honesty or authenticity, it was the only viable option. As he says later on in *De Profundis*: "Only that is spiritual which makes its own form" (197).

Note here Wilde's subtle but important shift away from the sensational aestheticism of Pater. In *The Renaissance*, Pater merely had drawn on the experience of universal mutability originally suggested by Hume, who had argued that the universe is nothing but a bundle of impressions, elements in a state of constant flux, combining and dissipating. The world, in this conception, is composed of merely unstable, flickering stimuli "which burn and are extinguished with our consciousness of them." Individual identity is no more than a "thick wall of personality" through which no real voice has ever penetrated. We can only conjecture as to what is without, each of us "keeping as a solitary prisoner its own dream of a world." Under the inconstant, fluctuating physical circumstances of life, art comes to us "proprosing frankly to give nothing but the highest quality to your moments as they pass, and simply for those moments' sake" (1128–29). But the "aesthetic moment" in Pater was something that he could not retrieve from the world of sensation himself. For, as Wolfgang Iser points out, to achieve such "a transcendental stance towards oneself would mean transcending the aesthetic existence."[3] Pater was never able to circumscribe a reality he conceived in empirical terms only. In the end, art is no different in essence from any other sensation.[4]

In Wilde's view, Kant showed the insufficiency of this empiricism because he taught that knowledge was not founded soley on experience of sensation but also on "the *thinking* of our sensations" (*ON* 128, emphasis added). In the *Notebooks* Wilde writes that although knowledge is founded on sense experience, it "is not all derived from those experiences[,] for the impressions of relation have a potential or a priori existence in us and by their addition to sense experience constitute knowledge" (164). Whereas Pater could look at art only from the perspective of the disintegrating physical forces of life, Wilde looks at life through the refining lens of art ("Life is terribly deficient in form," etc.). In Wilde, the aesthetic judgment against life becomes a moral one as well: life fails to live up to our spiritual capacity, as much as it botches its own narrative designs. It lacks correspondence of "form and spirit," just as it makes a mess of us emotionally. To imagine that we can realize our capacities, our "perfection," through life is a terrible mistake. By "life" Wilde here, as always, implies not only the inconstant physical circumstances of which we are a part, but also society and institutions—in short, the specific sociological reality that Pater largely ignores. Yet, at bottom, Wilde accepted

Pater's protean image of life. It was on this metaphysically condemned site that Wilde constructed his plays, dialogues, and, finally, his life as a work of art, affirming in each the incongruity and peril of the venture of doing so with his superb wit, which forms the essence, not the ornament, of his undertaking. It was Pater's acquiescent view of art, together with his solipsism, that Wilde rejected.

As Wilde further develops his idea of criticism and the "true critic" in the dialogue, the contradiction inherent in the question itself of the relation of "art" and "life" manifests itself even more clearly. The "first condition of criticism," he writes, "is that the critic should be able to recognise that the sphere of Art and the sphere of Ethics are absolutely distinct and separate." Yet a page later Wilde points out that "the artist . . . accepts the facts of life, and yet transforms them" in order to show "their true ethical import" (*I* 198–99). If art itself engages ethical truths, how can the spheres of "Art" and "Ethics" be "absolutely distinct and separate"? And if art concerns itself with ethics, why shouldn't criticism? Because, as Wilde puts it in another context, "The moral life of man forms part of the subject matter of the artist, but the morality of art consists in the perfect use of an imperfect medium" (*DG* x). The critic who focuses on the subject matter of art may therefore find much that is useful and true, but the true aesthetic critic is concerned with form ("the perfect use of an imperfect medium") because form, not subject matter, is the basis of art. In a utilitarian culture, form is what distinguishes art from all the other types of production that compete with it. There follows a passage on the centrality of form: it is the basis of dance and religion; it brings about "the birth of passion" and "the death of pain." It is in fact— and here the paradox is at its sharpest— "the secret of life" (*I* 208). The intimation of this secret, to which presumably the key ideas of "fate" and "prophecy" pertain, is as far as Wilde could take the ethical-aesthetic question, as it relates to the particular work of art, at this point in time; in *De Profundis* Wilde's understanding of "form" deepens further as he looks more carefully at its relation to his own life, and as the speculative theological context for the whole problematic comes to the fore (see chapter 4).

Wilde's statement on form, however, does not end the meditation on ethics and aesthetics in "The Critic as Artist." Wilde returns to it at the end of the dialogue: "Aesthetics, in fact, are to Ethics in the sphere of conscious civilization, what, in the sphere of the external world, sexual is to natural selection. Ethics, like natural selection, make existence possible. Aesthetics, like sexual selection, make life lovely and wonderful, fill it with new forms, give it progress, and variety and change" (*I* 221–22). In using the word "aesthetics" and the word "ethics" in plural form, Wilde implies that neither is an abstract system, and that both, as in Kierkegaard's *Either/Or,* represent a set of "norms," as it were, for living. Aesthetics are "higher than ethics," but not because ethics are subordinate—anymore than Darwin's "natural" selection is subordinate to a sexual selection indifferent to procreation; it is Wilde's main contention that ethics "make existence possible." (Ethics presupposes aesthetics as natural selection presupposes sexual preference.) What ethics cannot give to life, however, is "progress, and variety and change." Only aesthetics can do that.

Without the aesthetic, then, there can be no "higher ethics" (*I* 135), because it is from the aesthetic that the power to *progress* derives. The penetration and critique of conventional or "vulgar standard[s] of goodness," which is necessary to progress, is the work of the aesthetic imagination, and not, for example, "Humanitarian Sympathy."[5] Wilde learned this from both Plato and Ruskin, but whereas Plato eventually excludes all but a few poets from the state, and Ruskin insists that some kinds of art are moral and some are not, Wilde says that love of beauty itself is the beginning and end of all education: all efforts to deny aesthetics its proper role in the ethical realm will result in the deterioration of the ethical life of man.

As dangerous as the love of beauty can be—and Wilde, we have seen, never tired of pointing this out[6]—it is only aesthetic "criticism," not some "vague system of abstract ethics," that endows us with the cosmopolitanism that makes it possible to "rise superior to race-prejudices" (*I* 219). We cannot realize "the brotherhood of humanity" through any abstract doctrine of universal brotherhood, however attractive to the emotions such a notion is, but only through the cultivation of a critical understanding of other cultures and their traditions, such that those cultures become part of our own cultivation. In understanding the deep relation between cosmopolitan education and the political well-being of Europe, Wilde knew better than Arnold himself what the earlier critic meant when he remarked in *Culture and Anarchy* that "the men of culture are the true apostles of equality."[7] Whereas Arnold refers to equality of education among the English, in "The Critic as Artist" Wilde extends his meaning to include a political parity among nations made possible by the unifying spirit of cosmopolitanism.

As for the "ethical effect of art . . . its place in the formation of character," this "had been done once and for all by Plato" (*I* 120), from whom Wilde quotes at length in "The Critic as Artist."[8] A sense of beauty is absolutely essential to the development of one's ethical being, far more important than the abstract humanitarian or, in today's jargon, "humanistic" program, which inevitably "limits knowledge" because of its smiling emotionalism, "and so prevents us from solving any single social problem" (184). But Wilde never claims that the aesthetic sense automatically makes people good, only that the aesthetic sense, and the aesthetic sense alone, *can* make people truly good: "And when we reach the true culture that is our aim, we attain to . . . the perfection of those to whom sin is impossible . . . because they . . . wish for nothing that can do the soul harm" (222). That an immersion in art, or in aesthetic sensibility, can also make people bad is never denied. The shadows of Browning's Duke of Ferrara and James's Gilbert Osmond hover behind Lord Henry in *The Picture of Dorian Gray*. Like the later Tolstoi, Wilde was fully aware of the potentially corrupting effect of the aesthetic sense, its power to infect (the trope of "The Portrait of Mr. W. H."). Because life imitates art, such corruption is always possible. Nevertheless, the "spiritualising" and "purification" of human nature remains an aesthetic phenomenon. (Christ as an *artist* is Wilde's theme in *De Profundis*, even after he himself had suffered so terribly; Wilde rejected the doctrine of atonement). The purifying power of Aristotle's catharsis, he writes, is "essentially aesthetic" (121): that is, aesthetic in its essence and moral in its consequence. Only the aesthetic can initiate us into noble feelings, of which we might otherwise have known nothing, and rites of initiation are social and moral in character.

This does not mean that art teaches us virtues. "Virtues! Who knows what the virtues are? Not you. Not I. Not anyone. It is well for our vanity that we slay the criminal, for if we suffered him to live he might show us what we had gained by his crime. It is well for his peace that the saint goes to his martyrdom. He is spared the sight of the horror of his harvest." It follows then that "what is termed Sin is an essential element in progress." Approaching the antinomian ideas of his near-contemporary, Kierkegaard, Wilde suggests that in "its rejection of the current notions about morality," sin, or "what is termed Sin . . . is one with the higher ethics" (*I* 134–35). As Wilde was fond of recalling, Jesus preferred the company of sinners to that of respectable members of society because they offered more hope for the future of mankind.

Wilde is not here suggesting that we actively sin in order to progress; his position anticipates the *attitude* of Stephen Dedalus who says "*non serviam.*" Of action itself, Wilde is skeptical. "When man acts he is a puppet" (*I* 135). "Action! What is action? It dies at the moment of its energy. It is a base concession to fact" (138). It is only through the cultivation of inwardness, an aesthetic task, that we realize our perfection, our ethical perfection, if you will. This is why "The world is made by the singer for the dreamer," not the man of action (138). What Wilde calls "criticism" is the best means by which this inward cultivation can take place, above all because of its propaedeutic removal from "life." Whereas the creative artist can always appeal "from fact unto fiction," there is no appeal from the inwardness that aesthetic contemplation demands of us. The "highest criticism" is "the record of one's own soul," and "from the soul there is no appeal" (143–44).

The most "subjective" criticism therefore becomes the most "objective," the freest from the external world's influences and standards.[9] When pressed by Ernest to justify criticism or to explain the usefulness of so inward an activity as aesthetic contemplation, Gilbert simply remarks: "You might just as well have asked me the use of thought." By transcending things as they are, criticism not only "creates the intellectual atmosphere of the age" and "makes culture possible," it "makes us cosmopolitan" (I 215–18). It is the critical spirit alone that enables us to get beyond our own interest. As we see in the following comparison of Wilde and Nietzsche, there is no more distinguishing feature of Wilde's thought than this explicit affirmation of criticism. It was by means of this emphasis that Wilde developed the ethical dimension of his aestheticism and harnessed his devotion to pure art.

Wilde and Nietzsche

A comparison between Wilde and Nietzsche reveals Wilde's uniquely English response to a world situation. For Wilde stood at a point in history on which all the contradictory influences of the nineteenth century were brought to bear, and he was as conscious of representing this position as his contemporary on the continent was, to whom he was compared by both Gide and Thomas Mann. In fact Wilde and Nietzsche inherited the same situation in philosophy: what earlier in the century Engels had called the "despair of reason," its confessed inability to solve the contradictions with which it is ultimately faced. The flaunting of paradox in each writer (what Nietzsche early characterized as a consequence of "logic's biting its own tail") is a function of this despair as well as a bid to master it, just as their shared deployment of aphorism may be seen as a sign of resistance to enter any system.[10] Having lived through the last crisis of classical reason, each remained at bottom an aesthete, maintaining in the face of the prevailing utilitarianism of their countries a conviction that it is "through Art, and through Art only, that we realise our perfection; through Art, and through Art only, that we can shield ourselves from the sordid perils of actual existence" (Wilde, *I* 174); and that "We possess *Art* lest we *perish of the truth*" (Nietzsche, *WP* 435). It could be maintained that each man perished of the truth nonetheless, and that, as in some strange new mutation of the possibilities of tragic heroism, the madness and collapse of the one finds its pendant in the imprisonment and prostration of the other. Both could think of themselves at the end of their careers as the crucified one.[11]

Each a student of classical philology (Nietzsche at the universities at Bonn and Leipzig, Wilde at Oxford, under Müller), their aestheticism arose out of an engagement with the ancient world, though in neither case was it limited by the presuppositions of scientific linguistics. Wilde identified with classical Greece, Nietzsche with presocratic Hellenism; Wilde's patron God was Apollo, Nietzsche's was Dionysus. It may have been Wilde's sensuality and liberal upbringing that drew him as a young man to the ideal of measure, restraint, and harmony, of art and illusion in the service of "sweetness and light." Nietzsche's ascetic upbringing, by contrast, may have developed an opposing consciousness of the power of art to intoxicate. But both the Apollonian and the Dionysian are, as one critic has written, "art-solutions"[12]—one involving illusion, the other ecstasy—to the problem of living in a world without the comforts of faith, whether religious or scientific. Or the comforts of art. Existence is bearable, says Nietzsche, only if we become artists ourselves, not simply of works of art, but of our own lives. We must become "poets of our lives" (*JW* 233), each of us imitating the techniques of the artists, viewing oneself at a distance, and coming to see all the details of one's life as fitting together into a certain dynamic unity. Both *Ecce Homo* and *De Profundis* are concerned with this art of life, with what Nietzsche calls "becoming what one is." In coming to see the necessity of every detail of our past, in coming to love our own fate, agonistically, we become "who we are." The self is thus something discovered as well as something constructed. But this making, this architectonics of identity, is no simple matter, involving as it does a responsibility for the fundamental question of "what one is." For, given that we do not construct out of thin air but only out of some given—that is to say, historical—set of possibilities, who then is the "I" doing the constructing? What one normally takes for granted as (the) human being is at bottom a problem: a problem of "taking for granted." With its dogmatic emphasis on purely external, socially determined forces, or alternately on a conception of truth as mere consensus, with its programmatic conception of human identity and its overall institution of false security, its total administration, the bourgeois human agenda constitutes a *refusal* to become what one is, a repression of the fundamental existential questionableness. "One must never have spared oneself," writes Nietzsche in *Ecce Homo*, at an intellectual and spiritual juncture not entirely unlike that of Wilde in *De Profundis*; one must be "a monster of courage and curiousity" (*EH* 264), capable of the profoundest sacrifice. In this sense, one that effectively overcomes the dichotomy of Greece and Judea, Erich Heller characterizes Nietzsche, in words that could also be used to describe Wilde, as a "Christian of the aesthetic passion."[13]

Chapter 4 develops these ideas in detail: particularly, the idea that Wilde responded, both in his life and in his work, to the Kantian undermining of a truth in itself by developing an advanced aestheticism similar to, but also different in crucial ways from, that of Nietzsche. As an introduction to this undertaking, however, some preliminary points about the ethical implications of Wilde's aestheticism need to be made.

It should be obvious by now, for example, that Wilde's ambition to make his life into a work of art, though it may owe something to Pater's famous conclusion to *The Renaissance*, owes far less than has been supposed. For the task of becoming an artist of one's life is not the same as living in the "aesthetic state" of sensual receptivity, of "burn[ing] always with this hard, gemlike flame." In *De Profundis*, Wilde himself greatly broadens Pater's meaning when he uses Pater's strikingly romantic formula—that "failure is to form habits"—to explain the ethical failure of his relations with Douglas. For had Wilde been more faithful to Pater's vision in his relations with Douglas, taking "each moment only" at its full sensuous value, it is unlikely that he would have been able to contain the excesses of a relationship based largely on the sensual gratification Pater had extolled, let alone been able to discover the temporal significance of the experience as he does in *De Profundis*. To recognize the ugliness of Douglas's habitual hold over him was, for Wilde, as much an ethical as an aesthetic operation.

Wilde's early aestheticism is rooted more in the icy doctrine of Théophile Gautier than in the fervor of Pater,[14] and though he anticipates some of the extremes of Nietzsche's philosophy, he does not realize them himself. For satiric purposes, the immature Wilde pretended to believe what the young Nietzsche, as a product of German Lutheran society, once earnestly accepted: namely, that morality and bourgeois morality are the same. The great tradition of English moral criticism from Samuel Johnson, Austen, and Carlyle to William Thackeray and George Eliot, a tradition in which conventional morality is interrogated from a larger and deeper ethical ground, if not yet from the perspective of the "immoralist," would make it impossible for any man-of-letters in England, except the insouciant undergraduate wit, to maintain such an attitude, and Wilde enjoyed being an undergraduate wit for some time after he left Oxford. Nevertheless, his deep tie to the Victorians would determine the character of much of this thinking as essentially moral: that is, as centrally occupied with the moral failure of his age as it bore upon the ancient question of how to live. In "The Decay of Lying" Wilde does not use the word *fiction* in his title in place of *lying*, though literature is his subject; the argument is placed squarely in the context of the history of the moral life.

The speaker of the "The Decay of Lying," who seems to wish to live his entire life indoors, might take as his motto Yeats's line: "Once out of nature I shall never take / My bodily form from any natural thing." Yet Wilde's influence upon Yeats, whom he knew personally, and the association of his aestheticism with that of Nietzsche, has obscured the fact that, even in his earlier works, Wilde was never an *absolute* aesthete. The rejection of nature, of "this world" or the "real" world, that characterizes continental aestheticism and is rooted perhaps in a Christian vision of transfiguration (mediated through Arthur Schopenhauer), is paradoxically and parodically asserted in "The Decay of Lying" and other works, but, as Wilde matured, he would reject historical Christendom, above all in its *aesthetic* aspect. In "The Soul of Man under Socialism," as we have observed, Wilde represents Christ as one who realized "his perfection through pain" (*I* 333), but the evolution of society is now making that impossible. The great work of Christianity is ending, he suggests, and the social reformer Wilde draws back in moral and aesthetic distaste from what his countryman Samuel Beckett would later call, in Nietzschean vein, a "loathsome form of torture worship."[15] Nor does Wilde (going beyond Pater) embrace pleasure as the alternative: "For what man has sought for is, indeed, neither pain nor pleasure, but simply Life." "Life" here is neither simply pain nor simply pleasure; we have yet to realize it "except in Thought," as the Greeks did, and "except in Art" as the Renaissance did (334–35).

By "Life" Wilde here means existence in both thought *and* art, an intellectual and aesthetic ideal of living that is a practical basis for the social philosophy of "The Soul of Man under Socialism." This twofold ideal is often overlooked in received views of Wilde because he began his career as a celebrity by espousing the Pre-Raphaelite cult of beauty. Even in his earliest reviews, however, Wilde shows himself to be conscious of the limitations of *l'art pour l'art*. In a review of a lecture by Whistler of 1885, for example, he emphasizes the "wide difference" between the attitude of a painter towards his subject and "the attitude of a people towards art." The artist's ability to find beauty in the ugliness of modern life does not tell the whole story, as Whistler would have us believe. It is true that "under certain conditions," what is ugly can be made beautiful by the modern artist, "but these conditions are exactly what we cannot be sure of." There is still the question of the role of beauty in *life* to be considered, for "the arts are made for life, and not life for the arts." A life in which beauty exists as a living presence, and not just in the exhibited artwork of museums, should be "the natural and national inheritance of us all" (*M* 68–69, 71).

In the developed aestheticism put forth in "The Critic as Artist," Wilde moves beyond the contemplative ideal of a life lived in thrall to the "beautiful sterile emotions" of an art "which does not hurt us" to an idealist aestheticism that engages the real world:

> Unlimited and absolute is the vision of him who sits at ease and watches, who walks in loneliness and dreams. But we who are born at the close of this wonderful age are at once too cultured and too critical, too intellectually subtle and too curious of exquisite pleasures, to accept any speculations about life in exchange for life itself. . . . [F]or, just as Nature is matter struggling into mind, so Art is mind expressing itself under the conditions of matter, and thus, even in the lowliest of her manifestations, she speaks to both sense and soul alike. . . . Like Aristotle . . . we desire the concrete, and nothing but the concrete will satisfy us. (*I* 177–78)

These ideas are not to be confused with Pater's sanction of aesthetic sensation, which Wilde (in his review of Pater) found too "abstract" when applied to the subject of style or art (*R* 540). The passage affirms both theory *and* sensation—as the allusion to an Aristotelian immanent essentialism implies—and, if anything, suggests a release from the passivity of Pater's ideal of life. In contemplating art, the critic makes the unconscious conscious, and in discriminating the work that has distinction from that which does not, he perfects the culture of the future. Wilde's vision of the new artist-critic displays an ambition to overcome the opposition between abstract and concrete, criticism and creation, Apollo and Dionysus, an ambition akin to that of the early Romantics in Germany.

Increasingly conscious of this imperative to transcend the antitheses, Wilde shows none of the hysterical extremism normally associated with the fin-de-siècle aesthete. Jules Barbey d'Aurévilly's suggestion that the aesthete faces in the end either the foot of a cross or the muzzle of a gun suggests how far the classically balanced, coolly hedonistic Wilde was from the state of mind of other late romantics. On the continent, Otto Weininger recommended suicide in his best-seller *Sex and Character*; his own spectacular suicide at the age of twenty-four in the house where Beethoven died won Oswald Spengler's admiration for its "nobility." By contrast, Wilde's internal aplomb and outward composure in the face of public humiliation and prosecution, prison, disease, and early death are demonstrated again and again in the resourceful expression of his wit. Even on the courtroom stand, he could rarely be made defensive, but responded to over-simplified and baiting questions with intellectually suggestive replies. As his conviction loomed more certain, as he faced and endured imprisonment and exile, the moral attentiveness of his wit seemed actually to intensify.

Wilde's self-sacrifice to English law, which is taken up in more detail in the following chapter, must be seen in the context of his thought. In "The Soul of Man under Socialism" he writes of self-sacrifice in Nietzschean terms as a "survival of savage mutilation" (*I* 326). But unlike Wilde, Nietzsche glorifies self-sacrifice, saying in his critique of the Christian pacifism that the species survives only by human sacrifice. It may be that Wilde's sacrifice, which, as I shall argue, had for him a renewing moral and philosophical significance, exemplifies Nietzsche's idea. Yet in affirming the significance of his self-destructiveness in *De Profundis*, as Wilde clearly does, he does not glorify it. It is a sacrifice imbued with sorrow, not ecstasy. To one who pursued pleasure and satisfied desire with Apollonian serenity for most of his life, the notion of self-sacrifice betokened the "hideous cant" (326) of the Victorians. "It takes a thoroughly selfish age, like our own, to deify self-sacrifice" (185), writes Wilde in "The Critic as Artist." Frank Harris reported that one of the only times in which he ever saw Wilde get angry was when Harris presumed to urge upon him the moral benefit to be derived from his suffering in prison.

Yet Nietzsche's contemptuous attacks on the herd morality of the English, on their utilitarianism and debased, public-relations egalitarianism, on their bustling and desperate pursuit of happiness: all this was anticipated by Wilde, who said that most Englishmen live like "petted animals." What Wilde does not share with Nietzsche is the extreme anarchism that led the latter to glorify self-sacrifice, to denounce democratic institutions, and to recommend war. "One has renounced the *great* life when one renounces war" (*TI* 489), Nietzsche proclaimed. Culture can only be renewed by a certain barbarism, he insisted, and it is vain sentimentalism to think otherwise.

Wilde too detested sentimentalism but in his relentless attack on the sogginess of English ethics, he turns not to instinct but to intellect, as this key declaration makes perfectly clear: "The real weakness of England lies, not in incomplete armaments or unfortified coasts . . . but in the fact that her ideals are emotional and not intellectual" (*I* 187). To Wilde, ethics is rooted not in any barbarism, however sophisticated, but in an explicitly intellectual ideal, which is obscured by the idea of emotion. When Wilde says, therefore, that all "action . . . belongs to the sphere of ethics" (183), he is using the word "ethics" in a double sense: a philosophical sense alongside the sense commonly employed in Victorian literature. A further example of the philosophical use of the word may be found in this statement already cited: "Ethics . . . make existence possible. Aesthetics . . . give it progress, and variety and change" (221–22). Taking the sentence "Ethics make . . . existence possible" out of context, as aphorisms invite us to do, confers on it even more weight than it already has, imparting, for example, a peculiar spin to the word "possible." Ethics makes existence possible as such, in its existing, in which case ethics precedes existence in the manner of Platonic ideas; or ethics makes existence possible in the sense that it realizes it, makes it worthwhile, in which case the ethical is somehow simultaneous with the existential as, for Kant, the intelligible is simultaneous with the sensuous. This means that, before comprising any sublimation of brute facts or "interests," society is from the beginning, in its possibility, a matter of ideas.

Against this intellectualist definition of ethics is its own corruption in Victorian society, an ethical corruption that has come about through society's emotional obsessions and, as we shall see, its insensitivity to the role that aesthetics plays in ethical discovery. The "basis of the stability of [English] society . . . is the complete absence of any intelligence amongst its members." England's degraded conception of ethics elevates the "great majority of people . . . to the dignity of machines" (*I* 188). "Contemplation is the gravest sin of which any citizen can be guilty" (176). Not understanding that the sphere of ethics in the deepest sense is a matter of ideas that condition the practical domain, the Victorians have produced only a "nuisance of the ethical sphere" (186–87), the philanthropist, who believes that decisive action in itself signifies virtue and can propagate it. In its ignorance of the indispensable role of aesthetic experience in the development of virtue, Victorian civilization does nothing to develop "the simple and spontaneous virtue that there is in man" but only succeeds in destroying such virtue with "well-meaning and offensive busybodies" (188–89).

Unlike Nietzsche, who repeatedly sought isolation, and Pater, who lived at a distance from the practical world of political and ethical controversy, Wilde was drawn to social life and observed the Bourgeois Man of his time at close range. Whereas Nietzsche glorified the man of action (albeit an aristocratic action) over the bourgeoisie, Wilde saw that the bourgeois was nothing but unthinking action, and praised instead the contemplative man. With extraordinary perspicacity, Wilde wrote, "the one person who has more illusions than the dreamer is the man of action. . . . When man acts he is a puppet" (*I* 133, 135). He saw clearly the predatory character of the industrial magnate which Nietzsche tended to overlook in his assumption that the commercial, shopkeeping spirit was pacifistic. Wilde saw the spirit of commercialism behind war and imperialism. "The Manchester school tried to make men realise the brotherhood of humanity, by pointing out the commercial advantages of peace. It sought to degrade the wonderful world into a common marketplace for the buyer and seller. It addressed itself to the lowest instincts, and it failed. War followed upon war, and the tradesman's creed did not prevent France and Germany from clashing in blood-stained battle" (218).

Wilde writes, "There never was a time when Criticism was more needed than it is now" (*I* 215). Only criticism can educate emotion to its own oblivion, its own unacknowledged intellectual fundament. Only criticism can contend with the organized ignorance of modern democratic society, with its calculated public opinion elevated "to the dignity of physical force" (216). In truth, "It is Criticism that makes us cosmopolitan" (218), and, once again, it is only by "the cultivation of the habit of intellectual criticism that we shall be able to rise superior to race-prejudices." The "emotions will not make us cosmopolitan, any more than the greed for gain could do so" (219). "Criticism will annihilate race-prejudices, by insisting upon *the unity of the human mind* in the variety of its forms. If we are tempted to make war upon another nation, we shall remember that we are seeking to destroy an element of our own culture, and possibly its most important element. As long as war is regarded as wicked, it will always have its fascination. When it is looked upon as vulgar, it will cease to be popular." Wilde gives the example of Goethe, who was silent when called upon to write songs of hatred against the French during Napoleon's invasion of his homeland. How could I hate, said Goethe, "a nation . . . to which I owe so great a part of my own cultivation?" Intellectual criticism "will bind Europe together," Wilde concludes (219–20, emphasis added).

When one considers that Wilde grew up reading (and later reacting against) the great Victorian prose-writers for whom rationality yielded an imaginative spell stronger than the religion which formed their minds, and that the thinking of each of them would founder on this dilemma, namely, the excessive demands put upon human reason in the absence of religious faith; when one considers how little sympathy Wilde had from the beginning with the whole tradition of English positivist philosophy, compared with his awareness of (and radical sympathy with) the continuing specter of revolution in countries outside England from the late eighteenth century forward; when one considers, in short, how much cause Wilde had to question the whole tradition of Victorian moral criticism, as seen in chapter 2, it is a wonder that he was not drawn to a more violent aestheticism. This was one temptation to which he did not yield, however, and it makes all of his indulgences pale in comparison. Perhaps because Wilde's upbringing had none of the disabling, ascetic strictness found in that of some of his predecessors, like Carlyle, Ruskin, and Mill, not to mention Nietzsche, he had the power to alter the course of the rational tradition of English criticism. For him to write that "There was never a time when [Cosmopolitan] Criticism was more needed than it is now" (*I* 215), at any rate, tells us how right Pater was when he said that it was Wilde (not himself) who was Arnold's true heir. Like Arnold, Wilde insisted that the cosmopolitan critic be disinterested and refuse to bind himself to the "shibboleths of any sect or school" (220). But, unlike Arnold, Wilde insists that the state of mind that recognizes no position as final, the promotion of such intellectual freedom, is potentially dangerous. Indeed, "all ideas . . . are so" (222). In order to have "any true intellectual value" (188), an idea must transcend things as they are; by definition it challenges the status quo. To condemn an idea for being potentially dangerous shows a fundamental ignorance of "what thought really is" (187).

Wilde would not have been surprised, for example, by the Nazis' appropriation of Nietzsche's ideas. Because "Life imitates Art" such misinterpretation is always possible; in an uneducated or semieducated populace, it may be inevitable. There is a world of irony in Wilde's oft-quoted remark that he "lived in fear of being understood." On the one hand, it suggests foreknowledge that his ideas would be crudely imitated by well-meaning, uneducated minds; on the other, it suggests hope that his own work would be the starting point for a new creation, not simply a repetition of his own: an important element in Wilde's theory of how criticism operates through history. The Deleuzian "amalgam of forces . . . held apart from one another" in this aphorism has to do with the gap between Wilde's critical ideal and the brute sociological reality.

With regard to the so-called "politics" of Wilde's aestheticism, it is worth remembering that the aesthetic imagination, as Wilde actually defines it, is of course the least likely candidate for service to a political regime, because it recognizes no position as final and will not attach itself to the shibboleths of sect or school. In much current academic criticism on aestheticism, this claim to distance and disinterestedness is not taken at all seriously; it comes too close to the ideas of the now unfashionable Matthew Arnold, whose "disinterestedness," as we know, was compromised in its service to a nationalistic ideal of English civilization as well as to governmental repression of social agitation preceding the passage of the second reform bill. In laying claim to a disinterested play of the imagination, however, Wilde is very unlike his predecessor: Wilde never declares that such disinterestedness is intended to accomplish certain ends, though he is not without hope that it will; he is speaking of what the aesthetic imagination *is*: a cosmopolitan force in history that insists upon "the unity of the human mind in the variety of its forms," and the sole authentic means available to us in modern society for utopian social and personal development. Because philosophy is inadequate to this task (we can no longer "accept any speculations about Life in exchange for life itself"), and because formal religion as well is failing (we "have exhausted the faith-faculty of the species"), we require something that "speaks to both sense and soul alike." Only in the historically informal experience of art, which is "mind expressing itself under the conditions of matter," will we ever have a chance of advancing our civilization.

As notable an achievement in the history of culture as it is, Wilde's reassociation of sensibility was subsequently overshadowed: first by the absolute aestheticism of writers like Mallarmé and Joris-Karl Huysmans, and then by the politically motivated repudiation of aestheticism that came into its own in the forties and fifties of the twentieth century. In his late essay entitled "Nietzsche's Philosophy in Light of Recent History," for example, Mann meditated the "close relationship" between aestheticism and "barbarism," concluding that an "aesthetic ideology is absolutely unempowered to meet the problems we must solve."[16] We have seen how little Wilde's aestheticism conforms to this judgment. The "unbarbaric side of philosophy," to borrow a phrase from Theodor Adorno, lies precisely in its tacit awareness of its own freedom from what it judges.

4

§ Wilde's Philosophy of Art

"The Decay of Lying" and the Question of Truth

THE PUBLICATION of "The Decay of Lying" in January 1889 marked
the decisive turn toward philosophical criticism in Wilde's career.
The turn from poetry to prose, which resembles an earlier shift toward critical and cultural commentary on the part of Arnold, is itself a parody of that shift. All the denunciations of "modern symp-
toms of decay" published in the latter half of the century, from the
most elevated to the most fatuous, are its target. The title refers
specifically to the didactic essay within the dialogue, authored by
Vivian, entitled "The Decay of Lying: A Protest." The overtly didactic purpose of Vivian's essay is undermined by its amoral asser-
tions and ultimately negated by the dialogue form insofar as it calls
into question any univocal truth. Unlike Vivian's essay, the dialogue
itself is not a "protest"; Vivian's exaggerations invite correction.
(Later, in "The Critic as Artist," Gilbert would say, "When people
agree with me I always feel I must be wrong.") The decay of lying—
or of fiction, or of the love of art for its own sake—is not something to be "protested." "Trying to reform others," wrote Wilde,
quoting from Chuang-tzu, is "as silly an occupation as 'beating a
drum in the forest in order to find a fugitive' " (R 223). Vivian's
drum-beating, his high moral tone and self-congratulation (all re-
flecting what in another context Wilde would call "our national
habit of self-glorification" [R 537]), must be vanquished by means
of parody—an indirect reform perhaps—before the "new aesthetic"
can be announced.

Wilde is clearly in sympathy with Vivian, who is the spokesman of the new aesthetic in the dialogue. As later works will demonstrate more fully, he felt that the time had come for such an innovation; and even in this most whimsical of all of his prose works, a certain weight falls on the summary pronouncement at the end, highlighting its major elements. Here Vivian is like a lecturer before an audience of undergraduates, rising to his peroration. As playful as the summary sounds, however, Wilde's earnest wish to advance a new aesthetic gains the ascendancy over the parody of earnestness. And why? Because the treacherous philosophical problem of truth underlying the dialogue's deployment of paradox and parody cannot be kept in abeyance.

Most serious writers at the end of the nineteenth century, especially those who, like Wilde, had read Kant, were convinced that there is no eternal or absolute truth accessible to human reason. In his "antimonies of pure reason," Kant had shown that a proposition can be "true" from one point of view—religious or teleological—but not from another. Wilde, however, in "The Decay of Lying," can only skim over the problem of the paradoxical nature of truth, and he does so by allowing Vivian to exaggerate ("In fact the whole of Japan is a pure invention. There is no such country, there are no such people," etc.), so as to suggest that all general statement invites contradiction. This is as far as he is willing or able to go in order to qualify the "truths" of Vivian's utterance on the new aesthetic. Wilde was no doubt aware that the conclusion to "The Decay of Lying," in which Vivian sums up the main points of this new aesthetic, sounded as dogmatic as anything his opponents wrote on the subject of art, and that he is hanging by a thread over an immense philosophical and moral problem.

What we see happening in "The Decay of Lying," then, is something like the performance of a trapeze artist: our gaze remains focused on the performer himself rather than on the abyss below.[1] The success of the performance depends on our *not* looking below. The delight Wilde takes in the precariousness of his position is both disarming and deceiving. For Wilde is indeed in a treacherous position, as the future will show when the question of truth rises again during the trials that would lead to catastrophe for him. Moreover, such pleasure in paradox takes our attention away from the moral dimension of the work; as suggested earlier, Wilde knew that the success of reform depends after all on our *not* beating a drum in the forest to find a fugitive. At this stage in his development, Wilde was poised between his aesthetic and his moral intentions; he was bringing them into relation. In "The Decay of Lying," the trapeze artist and the moral reformer are operating in tandem.

In the second half of this chapter I return to the question of truth as it bears on the trials and the writing of *De Profundis*. For the present, I would like to explore the development of the "new aesthetic" itself, through which Wilde postponed grappling with the most vexing elements of the problem of truth—that is, until his life circumstances made it necessary for him to do so.

The context in which the new aesthetic makes its appearance in "The Decay of Lying" is a reading of the decline of art in modern culture. The "decay of lying" refers, again, to the decline in the value of fiction or storytelling, "the loss that results to literature in general from [the] false ideal of our time": "useful information." We have "sold our birthright for a mess of facts." The journalist is replacing the artist.[2] The spiritual atmosphere that stories, paintings, and music can foster, and are fostered by, declines directly in proportion to the rise in value of useful information. Insofar as meaning itself has come to be conceived in terms of information, art becomes "useless," never expressing "anything but itself." (The newspaper article usefully imparts information but in itself is an empty vessel, whereas the story or "lie" contains within itself its own concrete suggestiveness and power.) The first and most vexing principle of Wilde's aesthetic, then, that art is "useless," rises out of and must be seen in relation to his reading of modern culture. Wilde's assertion of the "autonomy" of art, of its independence from "life," paradoxically originates in an experience of late nineteenth-century consumer culture.

A few decades later Walter Benjamin would take up the comparison between art and information in a different context in his well-known essay, "The Storyteller." In what does an artful story reside, asks Benjamin in "The Storyteller"? In its freedom from explanation as one reproduces it.[3] Similarly, "What is a fine lie?" asks Wilde, "Simply that which is its own evidence" (*I* 6). However remote, in the first instance, Benjamin may seem from Wilde, "The Decay of Lying" and "The Storyteller" make the same observation from either side of World War I, the first in the shape of optimistic satire, the second in the form of melancholic rumination. In the story or lie, the "most extraordinary things . . . are related with the greatest accuracy, but the psychological connection of the events is not forced on the reader. It is left up to him to interpret things the way he understands them, and thus the narrative achieves an amplitude that information lacks."[4] Both Wilde and Benjamin feel this "amplitude" vanishing as the flat empirical-pragmatic domain of positive fact expands in importance.

A contradiction emerges at this point in Vivian's discourse. On the one hand, art and life represent two distinct and separate spheres of action. Art "never expresses anything but itself" (*I* 44). It has an "independent life . . . and develops purely on its own lines" (54). On the other hand, there is that in art which attracts life to it and gives life meaning. "Life gains from Art not merely spirituality, depth of thought and feeling, soul-turmoil or soul-peace" (34), but life can secretly "form herself on the very lines and colours of art." "Life imitates art. . . . Scientifically speaking, the basis of life—the energy of life, as Aristotle would call it—is simply the desire for expression, and Art is always presenting various forms through which this expression can be attained" (40–41). Life imitates art because of the "amplitude" and "germinative power" that art possesses, as Benjamin later phrases it. The amusing stories Wilde relates in "The Decay of Lying," stories of people who imitate characters and incidents in novels and poems, suggest (above all perhaps because these anecdotes are themselves stories) the thinness of life without art. The "facts" of life depend on art for the way we see them; life is art's "pupil." This mimetic-expressive, pedagogical relation is the germ of the theory of reception by which Wilde resolves the main contradiction of aestheticism—that is, the paradoxical separation yet interdependence of art and life.[5] Art expresses only itself, but in its very energy is one with the generative life force. The work of art is formally independent of daily life, yet our reception of it yokes it *to* life. In Nietzsche's words, "Art is the great stimulus to life." (*TI* 529).

It was Kant who decisively introduced the spectator into the concept of aesthetics, and we see Kant's influence on Wilde in this emphasis on reception, or creative reception. Kant is important to Wilde also in an area in which Wilde's thought contrasts with that of Nietzsche. In *On the Genealogy of Morals*, Nietzsche attacks Kant for envisaging the aesthetic state from the point of view of the spectator rather than that of the creator. Kant lacked an artist's nature, says Nietzsche; "*personal* . . . vivid authentic experiences, desires, surprises, and delights in the realm of the beautiful" (*GM* 104) were not available to him. As a result, he gives a false view of "the aesthetic state" as an attitude of disinterested contemplation, rather than what it was, a state of primal force, of intoxicated action and even violation. Wilde, in contrast, repeatedly makes the point that the artist does more than purely create, that he also reads and thinks critically. In "The Critic as Artist," Wilde would develop the Kantian theory of reception to the point where the creative and the critical faculties, the artist and the spectator, are no longer opposed but vitally dependent on one another: it is "the critical faculty that invents fresh forms. The tendency of creation is to repeat itself" (*I* 128). "The mere creative instinct does not innovate, but reproduces" (130). "Without the critical faculty, there is no artistic creation at all, worthy of the name" (125). These ideas have a direct bearing on Wilde's cosmopolitanism; as indicated earlier, his reviews of different national literatures emphasize the provinciality of works that embrace a revivalist ideology, one that merely urges the reproduction, rather than innovation, of forms. (In his own plays, Wilde would put these ideas into practice.)

When Wilde makes the case for criticism in "The Critic as Artist," he emphasizes the immediate need for criticism: "There was never a time when Criticism was more needed than it is now. It is only by its means that Humanity can become conscious of the point at which it has arrived" (215).[6] Contemplativeness, free play of mind, spontaneity, and dream are qualities that characterize the highest criticism, and they are closely allied to art, to acknowledging and ordering "the treasures of [our] treasure-house" (128). "There is no fine art without self-consciousness, and self-consciousness and the critical spirit are one" (126–27). The effective merger of the creative and the critical, which certainly recalls the program of the first generation of German Romantics, is carried forward in the writings of the artist-critic Benjamin as well. Benjamin would write with profound simplicity that "experience has fallen in value,"[7] by which he means that *art* has fallen in value, together with our critical understanding of the past. "Experience [*Erfahrung*] is indeed a matter of tradition, in collective existence as well as private life,"[8] writes Benjamin. In "The Critic as Artist" Wilde uses the word *imagination*, calling it "concentrated race experience," in much the way Benjamin uses the word *experience*. In "The Decay of

Lying" Wilde had suggested that when art falls in value, so too will "life." Both propose in this connection that the value of "art" and the value of "life" are interdependent.

Out of this theoretical initiative emerges each author's attention to the "art critic," who is the custodian of what Benjamin calls experience (or, perhaps more accurately, "long experience") and what Wilde calls "imagination." The increasing atrophy or "decay" of experience—in Benjaminian terms, once again, the "decline of aura"—is a reflection of the surrender of both art and criticism to information. To the extent that factuality is valued over art (and criticism), information over the older narration (and the "tradition" that older narration embodies), experience is emptied of content and the past turned to dust in our hands. In "The Critic as Artist" Wilde is centrally concerned with how this past can be made to live on in the present, in what Benjamin would call its "afterlife," and he sees the artist-critic as bearing both the burden and the pleasure of this responsibility: his "punishment" and his "reward" (*I* 224).

However distant Arnold may seem from Wilde, and indeed from Benjamin, his entire conception of culture as one in which art and criticism are intimately connected to our experience of life, and in fact determine its quality, makes for a crucial precedent. Earlier in the century Arnold had noted that, because of the decline of religion, more and more people were adopting art as a model for conduct and for interpreting life. Arnold's well-known and desperate solution to the ethical chaos that he supposes this would create is put forth in "The Study of Poetry," in an argument, among other things, for the need for firm literary and aesthetic standards of judgment: "More and more mankind will discover that we have to turn to poetry to interpret life for us, to console us, to sustain us. . . . [To] be capable of fulfilling such high destinies, [poetry] must be poetry of a high order of excellence. We must accustom ourselves to a high standard and to a strict judgment."[9] The "touchstone" method Arnold offers for keeping quotations in our minds that represent the highest standard of what has been thought and said—a substitute for dogmatic religion—constitutes a practical and moralistic application of traditional art that, whatever its relation to human conduct, will inevitably paralyze aesthetic standards. Arnold faintly acknowledges this problem when he points to the difficulty of using the touchstone method in judging contemporary art: "we enter on burning ground as we approach the poetry"[10] of our own time, he writes. It would be left to later aesthetes, symbolists, and philosophical critics, to develop the new aesthetic. Such an aesthetic, Arnold implicitly maintains, has to establish for *ethical* reasons the intentionlessness of art, as distinct from the strategic character of other forms of representation, such as the newspaper article, sermon, or political pamphlet. The so-called "autonomy" of art—the watchword of late-nineteenth-century aestheticism—is therefore the basis of its connection to life. Only by standing at a distance from life can art communicate to us "the true ethical import" of the "facts of life," as Wilde insists. Art's freedom from ethics is the basis of its usefulness to us as ethical beings. Its transcendence of received morality is what forwards our own ethical discovery.[11]

Wilde was never a serious proponent of what Benjamin calls the "negative theology of art" (as is, for example, Mallarmé), which totally denies any social function of art. Though he publicized the theory of art for art's sake in a period in which mechanical reproduction had begun to threaten the uniqueness of the work of art, Wilde was too much of a student of Ruskin to exclude social context from his theory of art's place and power. For *l'art pour l'art*, writes Benjamin, "was scarcely ever to be taken literally; it was almost always a flag under which sailed a cargo that could not be declared because it still lacked a name."[12] Wilde's aestheticism teaches that, although situated in its particular time and place, the work of art nonetheless possesses an inherently irreducible quality. The pine tree and the palm each grow in a particular climate, but this cannot wholly account for the living beauty of each. Still, the rootedness of the work in its epoch is essential to its human significance and to its distinctive effect throughout its afterlife. (In "The Truth of Masks," for example, Wilde argues that Shakespeare's plays must be performed in period costume if the metaphysical truth they possess is to be conveyed.) This aesthetic does not then return us to an eighteenth-century apparatus of universals but calls for a new attention to the historically situated and historically propagated work of art. From the time of his lectures in America, Wilde was working with these ideas:

> I will not try to give you any abstract definition of beauty—any such universal formula for it was sought for by the philosophy of the eighteenth century—still less to communicate to you that which in its essence is incommunicable, the virtue by which a particular picture or poem affects us with a unique and special joy; but rather to point out to you the general

ideas which characterise the great English Renaissance of Art in this century, to discover their source, as far as that is possible, and to estimate
their future as far as that is possible. (*M* 243)

Although Pater did not believe that art has an "essence" that separates it from sensuous experience in general, and although he was
not greatly interested in the "source" of art in the sociological sense
Wilde intends above—later in the lecture Wilde identifies the
French Revolution as "the most primary factor [in the] production"
of the English Renaissance—Pater's influence is discernible in this
passage. In *The Renaissance*, Pater had written, "To define beauty,
not in the most abstract but in the most concrete terms possible, to
find not its universal formula, but the formula which expresses most
adequately this or that special manifestation of it, is the aim of the
true student of aesthetics."[13] The critic who emerges with this new
aestheticism possesses above all the proper *temperament* for process-
ing new forms and impressions.

The Work of Art in a Postindustrial Age: *The Picture of Dorian Gray*

Wilde's theoretical investigation of the reception of works of art is
carried on in a piece published seven months after "The Decay of
Lying" (although probably written before it). Another experiment
in artistic criticism—an analysis of Shakespeare's sonnets is rather
uncomfortably encased in a tall tale—"The Portrait of Mr. W. H."
may be seen as an essentially Keatsian meditation on art, one that
first of all takes up the historical context of the work, then moves on
to consider its beauty and its effect upon its audience, past and present. The story begins with questions relating to the identity of
W. H., the person to whom Shakespeare dedicated the sonnets.
Who was this mysterious W. H.? Did he actually exist? These are
the sort of naive historical questions asked in our initial response to
a work of art: "What men or gods are these? What maidens loth?"
In the end the question of the historical identity of W. H. ceases to
be of interest and is surmounted. Interpretations arise from the sonnets themselves—that is, the sonnets as read—and they pass like a
virus from one reader to the next. No sooner has one reader (or
character) passed an interpretation on to another than he ceases to
believe it himself. It has flown, like the nightingale in Keats's ode,

and he is left wondering whether he wakes or sleeps. The spell that art casts is broken once our interpretation of it has crystallized: that is, once we too have created something. In the story, this creative-destructive crystallization is marked by the transmission of the interpretation to another.

The spell that emanates from the work and settles over the lives of the characters, in the faintly mocking "The Portrait of Mr. W. H.," becomes, in *The Picture of Dorian Gray*, the powerful aura called forth by the work of art. Benjamin would later describe the "aura" of the artwork as a "semblance of distance," however near, something which animates the presence of the object as though it were looking back at us.[14] ("His own soul was looking out at him from the canvas," Wilde writes of Dorian as he gazes at the painting [192].) The story of Dorian's life illustrates the dynamic by which this aura is realized in the world we know: novel and literary criticism become one. Whereas "The Portrait of Mr. W. H." leaves us uncertain as to what form we have encountered—short story? literary analysis? spoof? mystery?—in *The Picture of Dorian Gray* the romantic idea of criticism is at last fulfilled: a work of criticism becomes an autonomous work of art, as Friedrich Schlegel had demanded it should be, and as Wilde had wanted it to be in both "The Decay of Lying" and "The Portrait of Mr. W. H." Benjamin's own critical procedure would designate the work of art as "completed" by criticism, but also "annihilated" or "mortified" by it. *The Picture of Dorian Gray* is one of the first works to explore the modern "destructive" relation to art such as Benjamin would invoke. When, near the end of the novel, Lord Henry declares that "Art is a malady" (315), he refers not least, and by no means purely negatively, to what modern secular society has done to our experience of art.

The story of Dorian's relation to his own portrait is an intricately worked parable of the process of both depletion and expansion that can occur when we give ourselves to a work of art, the increase in our vulnerability to experience, the coming-to-life of the work of art, and the different ways we may react to and against art when all of this happens. In short, *The Picture of Dorian Gray* is about the dangers and opportunities that had arisen in a world in which art is no longer dependent on ritual. In this disenchanted world, the art object has achieved a life of its own, a nonritualized, nontraditional, magic that demands its human victims as once upon a time the ancient cult had done. In *The Picture of Dorian Gray*, the tendency to keep the painting private, to own it, even to hide it, suggests a sacralizing and fetishizing power from which we can never fully protect ourselves, just as Dorian cannot resist returning to the locked room where the painting is hidden and gazing upon it.

The story opens on a world Arnold predicted would come into being: a world without formal religion where art has become the central inspiration for conduct and for interpreting life among the characters. Here, in the figures of Lord Henry, Dorian, and Basil, we encounter "the critical and cultured spirits" of the future to whom Wilde alludes in "The Critic as Artist," those who "seek to gain their impressions almost entirely from what Art has touched" (*I* 164–65). Wilde situates them in a world of urban wealth and self-conscious connoisseurship, of exquisite sensibility and surfeited appetite. The studio in which the opening scene takes place is full of ornamental objects, such as Persian saddlebags and small Japanese tables, objects ransacked from faraway places, and at its center stands a painting. Dispossessed of any communal function, the work of art is thus a privately owned and privately experienced collector's object, elaborately ensconced in its allegorical arbitrariness.

What frees the work from purely solitary existence, however, is first of all dialogue. The opening scene, and much of the novel as a whole, is taken up with such dialogue, revolving about art and aesthetic experience in general, a dialogue restlessly and lightly pursued at every level of the narrative and never quite abandoned. It brings to mind Gide's recollection of the sense of mortal obligation Wilde always carried with him:

> But no sooner alone he would begin: "What have you done since yesterday?" And as my life at that time flowed along rather smoothly, the account that I might give of it offered no interest. I would docilely repeat trivial facts, noting, as I spoke that Wilde's brow would darken.
>
> "Is that really what you've done?"
>
> "Yes," I would answer.
>
> "And what you say is true!"
>
> "Yes, quite true."
>
> "But then why repeat it? You do see that it's not at all interesting. Understand that there are two worlds: the one that *is* without one's speaking about it; it's called the *real world* because there's no need to talk about it in order to see it. And the other is the world of art; that's the one which has to be talked about because it would not exist otherwise."[15]

It is in this sense, characteristic for modernity, that the painting is first brought into being in *The Picture of Dorian Gray*: by language. The covenant Dorian himself makes to trade his soul for eternal youth is a spoken covenant. "Words! Mere words! How terrible they were!" Dorian thinks in an earlier scene, "One could not escape from them" (30). Whoever enters into relation with a work of art, whoever gives himself or herself over to it, is then subject to the new life springing from it. Literally, the work of art does not come to life until it is appreciated or "re-cognized," as it were. Those who take it up with an open mind fall under its spell. But the spell manifests itself in different ways. Lord Henry wants to own the painting: "I will give you anything you like to ask for it. I must have it," he says (40). He is every type of collector or connoisseur whose relation to the object is that of obsessive voyeur. Hallward, the artist who painted the picture, has a less intimate or less intense relation to it. He produces it and gives it out, separating it from himself, and in the end he is the least responsible for the damage it causes. Late in the story, when he senses the harm that has come from the picture, he wants it *back*, which implies that his bond with it has never been as strong as that of the other characters. It is suggested that the painting is Hallward's only masterpiece, the one work in which he both drew on tradition and yet emancipated himself from it, rendering the subject for the first time in a contemporary way, rather than by means of traditional markings and associations. The work then is to be taken as a masterpiece of contemporary life and Dorian is the spectator that it mirrors: "It is the spectator, and not life, that art really mirrors," Wilde states in the preface (xi). In the story of what happens to Dorian, as I have suggested, Wilde explores the paradoxical loss and gain that occurs when we moderns give ourselves to a work of art. Our ethical norms, whatever they may be, tend to pale before the experience of the "fiery-colored world" illuminated by art. Dorian becomes increasingly curious about experiences that lie outside the norms he has known. The painting has burdened him with this new consciousness of life at the same time that *it* bears the burden of this consciousness; for Dorian's new life is not etched on his face but mirrored in the physiognomy of the portrait.

During the epoch in which the painting is created and viewed (Dorian's lifetime), it functions as a mirror, unavoidably telling the age the "truth" which the age itself wishes to deny, unconcealing that which is already present and hidden in the spectator. As Dorian says, it is "the visible emblem of conscience" (146). In response to its own collective image, then, the age, as represented by Dorian, begins to fear and despise itself, eventually submitting itself to total-ized control: Dorian places the painting under lock and key. When Dorian's act of censorship fails because, though hidden from public inspection, it cannot for long be hidden from his own, he tries to alter the painting, in the direction of the inoffensive, by reforming himself. The result, however, is only an upsurge in irony, a grim and unremitting anatomizing of self-deception: "He could see no change [in the portrait], save that in the eyes there was a look of cunning, and in the mouth the curved wrinkle of the hypocrite" (358). Ultimately, in this investigation of the strange, spiritual transformation secretively worked in the face of art, Dorian appre-hends the painting more and more crudely, and more and more willfully, as "evidence," as a document of his own guilty past; and for that reason, he tries to destroy it. But in destroying it, he inevitably destroys himself, with which development the novel neatly arrives at the central point of Wilde's moral-political aesthetic: "Art is a symbol, because man is a symbol" (*DP* 204). If you destroy art, you destroy humanity. Like Sybil Vane, who dies when she ceases to be able to create art on the stage, Dorian perishes the moment he sev-ers his relations to art.

When the age that the work has mirrored eventually passes (symbolically, when Dorian dies), it ceases to offer its image for im-mediate reflection and recedes into itself, becoming in its various aspects historical possibility, that is, more or less recognizable at some future moment when such possibility can be appropriately— "prophetically," in Wilde's terms—realized. As the contemporary context disappears, becoming at first more distant than the distant past, it throws the work which it occasioned into peculiar relief; or, in the words of Helen Vendler: "As the culture ideologically sup-porting a work decays, the work becomes 'merely' (merely!) beauti-ful."[16] Thus, after Dorian's death the painting is restored to its orig-inal beauty: "When they entered, they found hanging upon the wall a splendid portrait. . . . Lying on the floor was a dead man, in evening dress, with a knife in his heart. He was withered, wrinkled, and loathsome of visage. It was not till they had examined the rings that they recognized who it was" (362). The spectator, audience, or public now recognizes the painting in a new way, but do not at first recognize Dorian. That is: the historical context has now become unfamiliar, and the work of art recognizable as an enduring monument. As time passes, the material arrangements of society come to seem strange and the truth of *art* becomes familiar, an idea that brings us back to Benjamin's interpretation of the concept of fame: his plausible suggestion that the authentic artwork possesses an "after-life" or is intermittently reborn into subsequent history only after its material content—the immediate reflection of its epochal provenance—obtrudes on our attention, demanding interpretation as something obsolete.

Even while the work lives within its own particular epoch, its relation to the human soul or to the soul of the world around it is uncanny: "His own soul was looking out at him from the canvas" (*PG* 192). Seducing the soul, offering the soul a home outside of the self, it both depletes and extends that self; Dorian is deprived of both "real joy" and "real sorrow," experiencing only "the passion of the spectator" (252). The painting both preserves and annihilates his soul, imprisoning him in what Benjamin would later call a "dialectical image": near and familiar yet strange and remote, a marketable commodity yet a sacred presence, fixed yet mutable, contained yet open, dead yet alive. Bound to this collision of opposites by the covenant of language, Dorian cannot free himself from the painting any more than the self can exist without the soul. Art is a burden and a reproach ("it had to bear the burden that should have been his own," 226) and a reminder of what is lost, forgotten, and defiled in the process of living. Here is Arnold's idea of poetry as a "criticism of life" fully developed. As T. S. Eliot suggested years ago, the aesthetic movement was in the final analysis concerned with a theory of ethics, not simply with art but with art *in* life.[17]

The Politics of Reception

Given that in *The Picture of Dorian Gray* Wilde had shown that our relation to works of art is the measure of our spiritual sickness or health, his turn in the immediate aftermath of this venture to an explicit concern with politics was perhaps as inevitable as that of his teacher, John Ruskin. The relations between art and social class had already received attention in the novel. There Wilde shows that if the most conscious members of the educated and aristocratic classes exist in a competitive relation to art and try to dominate it, the working class unknowingly imitates art and is therefore dominated by it. Sybil, James, and Mrs. Vane all live out their personal lives in the thrall of either melodrama or tragedy. Sybil performs the role of Juliet in her own life, as she has on stage, when she kills herself; and James Vane, the embodiment of working class *resentment*, invites his own comically meaningless death when, as the Avenging Brother, he tries to hunt down his sister's seducer. (Vane himself is accidentally shot, together with a rabbit, during a shooting-party at Dorian's country estate.) To the inauthenticity of their lives is added a touch of corruption in their mother, who melodramatically performs her grief at her daughter's inquest.

In "The Soul of Man under Socialism" Wilde looks forward to a wider, more plastic interaction between the soul of man and art, and his focus is on the class of the future, the middle class. Published only eight months after *The Picture of Dorian Gray* first appeared in a magazine, the essay now develops the novel's concerns in the context of contemporary politics. The earlier focus on Dorian's particular relation to the painting ("I am jealous of the portrait. . . . Why should it keep what I must lose? Every moment that passes takes something from me, and gives something to it," 42) expands in the political essay to a focus on the English middle-class audience's demands that art be useful by promoting its values and sympathies. This open and crude demand for identification with art is Wilde's main concern. Popular art of a kind "that the public calls healthy," writes Wilde, "is always a thoroughly unhealthy production," indulging "the egotism of [its] ignorance, or the egotism of [its] information" (*I* 310, 318). In *Dorian Gray*, as we saw, the work of art comes to be kept under lock and key, a metaphor for the imposition of the spectator's ideas on art (as well as his fetishizing enthrallment *to* the art object); in "The Soul of Man under Socialism" Wilde explicitly warns, "the spectator is not to dominate the work of art" (317) but instead to cultivate a temperament receptive to it. Art's inherent but precarious immunity from the tyrannizing of the spectator is synonymous with human spiritual freedom and is truly possible only in a society that has passed beyond socialist materialism, a reconstructed society no longer preaching utilitarianism, nationalism, or the Christian ideal of self-realization through pain. As earlier chapters have shown, the artistically receptive spectator who can see this "dawn before the rest of the world" (224), and even help to bring it into being by his cosmopolitan character and concerns, is at the center of "The Critic as Artist."

Wilde's aestheticism at this point has made crucial advances in its meditation of the idea of receptivity, which he conceives, once again, as an *activity* that must be cultivated in the spectator of works of art. In "The Soul of Man under Socialism" Wilde singles out the audience of English drama as the population most in need of reform in this respect.[18] "The degrading effect of the public interest in the arts" had been most revealed in the creation of "silly, vulgar plays." "No spectator of art needs a more perfect mood of receptivity than the spectator of a play" (*I* 319). Not surprisingly, the creative medium to which Wilde now turned was drama and, after briefly trying his hand at tragedy with *The Duchess of Padua* and *Salomé*, he found his home in comedy, in particular a cross between the comedy of manners and that most moist of forms, Victorian melodrama. Strictly following his own dictum that it is the tendency of creation to repeat itself (and the tendency of criticism to develop new ideas), he wrote three remarkably similar plays before producing *The Importance of Being Earnest*. *Lady Windermere's Fan*, *A Woman of No Importance*, and *An Ideal Husband* all read as early drafts of *The Importance of Being Earnest*, as though Wilde was obsessively testing the limits of his ideas so as to emancipate himself (and his audience) from them. They illustrate more than anything else the critical impulse in Wilde's development as a playwright.

The artistry of each play and the place they hold in the histories of English and European theater, matters fundamental to any study of their meaning, have been extensively treated by other critics.[19] Wilde's achievement as a cosmopolitan artist is no doubt most evident in *Salomé*, in which the influences of Maurice Maeterlinck and the French symbolists are far-reaching and decisive. Derived from Gustave Flaubert's *Herodias* and composed first in French, this play moves furthest from English tradition, but the first three comedies reveal foreign influences as well. In them Wilde revised the traditional form of English melodrama through imitation of French and Norwegian models, thereby exemplifying Voltaire's description of the cosmopolitan artist who "obtain[s] kindling from our neighbors" and then "light[s] our own fire with it." The construction of the comedies was varied by using ideas of the *pièce bien faite*, in which the plot is a "seesaw of surprise and peripeteia" typically set in motion by various stage properties, such as fans, letters, or jewelry.[20]

Their unconventional moral emphasis—for example, the debunking of domestic ideology—came in part from working Henrik Ibsen's innovations into comic form, as Kerry Powell has shown. The creation of these plays was guided by a critical exploration of dramatic ideas that finally realized its aims in *The Importance of Being Earnest.*

With regard to the theoretical experimentation at issue in this chapter, the ideas that would prove most relevant to his development are to be found in Wilde's various meditations on art's relation to Christianity in "The Soul of Man under Socialism." There he suggests, much like Nietzsche, that Christian morality is by and large a symptom of cultural decadence. Based, we have said, on an ascetic ideal of self-realization through suffering, this morality finds its high point in the medieval art that Ruskin had extolled: "Medievalism, with its saints and martyrs, its love of self-torture, its wild passion for wounding itself, its gashing with knives, and its whipping with rods—Medievalism is real Christianity, and the medieval Christ is the real Christ" (*I* 331). Jesus made no attempt to restructure society, and consequently the ecstatic individualism he practiced and preached "could be realized only through pain or solitude" (330–31), the morality only through sacrifice. Once poverty and suffering have been done away with by socialism, however, a new moral ideal will emerge. "Pain is not the ultimate mode of perfection. It is merely provisional and a protest. It has reference to wrong, unhealthy, unjust surroundings. When the wrong, and the disease, and the injustice are removed, it will have no further place. It will have done its work. It is a great work, but it is almost over" (334). Under the new social circumstances socialism will create, Wilde implies that a new art will come into being, one based on pleasure rather than martyrdom. It is this kind of art (intimately tied up with Wilde's ideal of nonalienated labor) that he is aiming to achieve in the plays. Although *Salomé* is of biographical interest, as I have indicated, it is clear from "The Soul of Man under Socialism" that Wilde's sensibility was moving at this point in his career— that is, before Reading Gaol—beyond tragedy and the idea of self-realization through suffering. (He would revise his estimate of Christianity in *De Profundis.*)

The Victorian stage was steeped in a melodrama that Wilde looked upon not as amusing kitsch, and not as popular evasion of realistic truth, but as an accurate representation of the national sensibility: that "vulgar standard of goodness" that only the aesthetic imagination could penetrate. This sensibility was fundamentally Christian in character, and melodrama was its perfect expression because of the structure of crisis-resolved-through-sacrifice intrinsic to it. Each of the three comedies preceding *The Importance of Being Earnest* both conceals and reveals this structure. All of its components—the hidden past, the idealistic heroine, the self-sacrificing mother, the fallen woman—are firmly in place in each play yet are satirized in Wilde's brilliant epigrammatic raids on the prostitution of the emotions that they foster: "If a woman really repents," says Mrs. Erlynne in *Lady Windermere's Fan*, "she has to go to a bad dressmaker, otherwise no one believes her."[21] Such lines beat like butterfly wings against the Christian Victorian edifice of the action, making the audience laugh again and again at the very conventions supporting the play's structure. "Only in humor can language become critical," writes Benjamin. Through mining the *language* of Victorian melodrama by means of humor, Wilde developed in himself and in at least some of his audience, presumably, a critical relation to its structure. Ultimately, through these three experiments, the soggy form of melodrama is sublimated into the light, high, and dry comedy of *The Importance of Being Earnest*. At the center of this transformation is a rejection of what at this stage in his development, once again, Wilde identified as a Christian aesthetic. But the audience that could accept this rejection, announcing its acceptance through its laughter, was one that had already been educated by the three earlier plays.

The first stage in this revaluation of values takes place in *Lady Windermere's Fan*, in which Wilde plays with concepts of fate and character. As Benjamin points out in the essay "Fate and Character," character is usually placed in an ethical context, fate in a religious one. "We must banish them from both regions by revealing the error by which they were placed there. This error is caused, as regards the concept of fate, through association with that of guilt." The concepts of fate and character are inseparable, yet how do we theorize their difference when fate is always associated with guilt, suffering, and misfortune and character with both innocence *and* guilt? "Happiness and bliss are therefore no more part of the sphere of fate than is innocence,"[22] writes Benjamin, throwing into question the relations between fate and character, between fate and guilt, and between character and ethics. These relationships are also thrown into question in *Lady Windermere's Fan*: In so far as she is innocent, Lady Windermere can have no fate; at the end of the play, Wilde confirms her innocence by denying her a fate (knowledge of her mother's character is kept from her and she does not suffer). But this confirmation of innocence is wholly formal; it has no basis in *character*, since we already know Lady Windermere to be simply inexperienced and egotistical. At the same time that Lady Windermere is thus artificially granted innocence by being denied a fate, her mother, Mrs. Erlynne, is artificially granted guilt by being given a fate; yet her *character* rejects it. She has no "ambition" to suffer and be a mother, she declares, quickly shedding the burden of sacrifice: "I have no ambition to play the part of a mother. Only once in my life have I known a mother's feelings. That was last night. They were terrible."[23] In this way, the ties between character and fate are being thrown into question, and character is being liberated from its traditional ethical context. And all of this is accomplished through laughter. As the plot proceeds along conventional lines, the audience is made to laugh at the characters' constrained relation to it, deriding its own expectations and coming upon them as illusions.

The same uneasy relation between character and fate, or character and plot, is found in *A Woman of No Importance* and *An Ideal Husband*. In both of these plays the relation of character to ethics and fate ("I am bad because I have a sinful past. Bad things are going to happen to me because of it") is all but nullified; in the thoughtful, unconventional conclusion to *An Ideal Husband*, the guilty Sir Robert Chiltern retains both his good wife and his good name. And the Dandy, Lord Goring, delivers the moral message of this outcome in a statement that has often puzzled critics for its seeming support of a reactionary political stance we know Wilde did not take: "A man's life is of more value than a woman's" because it has "larger issues, wider scope, greater ambitions." Rather than make politics conform to her high moral standards, Goring declares, wives should simply love and support their husbands. In other words, given the institutions of government and marriage as they are, this is the most we can expect, the closest to an "ideal" that we can hope to achieve: corrupt but not wholly bad leaders, who can sometimes be redeemed and kept from further misdoing by the forgiveness of their blind, accepting wives. It is no wonder that Lord Goring, according to the stage directions, must pull "himself together for an effort"[24] to deliver this message, as though he is tired to death of the pontificating role that he—as dandy, wit, and aesthete, no less—is unreasonably required to play. A similar character appears in each of the earlier plays (it is the only character for whom Wilde feels any real sympathy), and this is the first and last time he is given the closing lecture. In *The Importance of Being Earnest*, Wilde is kind to himself at last. Removing this character from the morally unattractive company he is forced to keep, Wilde places him in a world in which all of the characters are dandies, worldlings, and wits, lightly richocheting off one another like so many helium balloons in the air. "Simpler, easier, higher, gayer": Konstantin Stanislavsky said these words ought to be inscribed on the front of every theater; and they are the words that should be inscribed on the text of *The Importance of Being Earnest*, a text in which a Christian aesthetic is momentarily transcended, but that contains within itself a tacit awareness of its own irresponsibility.

To summarize briefly, then: "The Soul of Man under Socialism" shows Wilde's interest in creating an art based on pleasure; but to create such art, Wilde suggests, one must transcend the Christian ideal of self-realization through pain. In drama, particularly, one must separate character from fate, because fate is what establishes character in pain, misfortune, crisis, and suffering. Wilde's rejection of Christianity—in the particular historical sense in which he defines it in "The Soul of Man under Socialism," as contrasted with *De Profundis*, where he would argue a clearer distinction between Christianity and Christendom, between the life of Christ and that of the church—is felt in these plays in his progressive undermining of ideas of fate as they relate to character. The dandy, who appears in the first three plays (one principal dandy in each play) is there to remind Wilde of what he is after. The dandy has no fate because he has no character.

In the cast of dandies of *The Importance of Being Earnest*, then, no one suffers and no one sacrifices. The nursery-room atmosphere of *The Importance of Being Earnest*, in which the worst sin is the eating of muffins and its biggest threat the arrival of the nanny, Lady Bracknell, takes us into the world of later Victorian nonsense of Edward Lear and Lewis Carroll, as critics of the play have noted. In more recent years *Monty Python* has recourse to Wilde's comic ideas, especially the idea of "going too far." Like the businessmen in *Monty Python* who become carried away by "putting one thing on top of another," all of the characters in *The Importance of Being*

Earnest go too far, like children acting up in the nursery, even to the point of performing their own baptism. The characters' notion of the rituals of life—of birth, baptism, and marriage—is entirely childlike and literal-minded, preoccupied only with form, with neatly arranging the surface of the gameboard so that the play can continue.

The plot of *The Importance of Being Earnest*, as Wilde knew, reflects the national myth of the century: the story of a person who was orphaned and who therefore is unsure of his name or identity, who eventually learns his true parentage and name and who can therefore have a new beginning, as in a baptism, and marry. Whereas in the earlier plays, the pieties lodged in this myth are overturned by epigrams alone, both epigrams and action perform this function in *The Importance of Being Earnest*.

The central piety here is that of social determinism, the idea that we are built up by the influence of the environment and that our past determines the course of our lives. We are who we are as a result of the unchangeable covenants made early in life, like Pip's covenant with the criminal, Magwitch, in *Great Expectations*. But in *The Importance of Being Earnest* everything, the past above all, can be repaired. Algernon and Jack even go back to their own christenings. Ernest, a character who never existed, dies and is brought back to life, and no one bats an eye. The arrival of the supposedly dead Ernest mirrors every character in Victorian fiction who, like Raggles or Magwitch, returns to haunt the present and to confront the main character with the question of who he is: who is the real Ernest? But being Ernest and being earnest can never coincide because of the relative insincerity required of us to live in society. When the two are brought together, the play ends.

In *Lady Windermere's Fan*, Victorian morality was reduced to a trivial object, a fan, which is an object of conspicuous consumption, a screen, and a beautiful thing. "The artist is the creator of beautiful things," wrote Wilde in the Preface to *The Picture of Dorian Gray* (ix). In the dandyish aestheticism of *Lady Windermere's Fan*, language and art are screens. In *A Woman of No Importance*, which concerns itself with the unmasking of stereotypes, the "reality" beneath them is exposed. But in *The Importance of Being Earnest*, the surface of language is presented to us as the only reality and the play *appears* to be celebrating the self-sufficiency of language in itself. It could be argued that the characters are mere assemblages of words or witticisms and that the language of the epoch speaks them, not the reverse. For at the same time that nothing is determined in the play's action—so different from the deployment of action in the Victorian novel—everything here is determined by language. Cecily is engaged to be married to Algernon three months before they meet: "You can see the entry if you like,"[25] she assures him, pointing to her diary.

In this vibrating linguistic universe, "The only really safe name is Ernest,"[26] says a character, wisely concerned with safety. In order to participate in the society or its institutions, such as marriage, some claim to a consistent identity must be made so that we may recognize one another, literally by *name*. Knowing this (in a play in which all of the characters are so innocently knowing), Jack and Algernon seek to establish themselves in the hearts and minds of the women characters by means of baptism, the naming ritual. It would seem that in the world of play "there is no event or thing . . . that does not in some way partake of language. . . . We cannot imagine a total absence of language in anything."[27] Wilde playfully anticipates Benjamin's philosophy of language (in "The Critic as Artist" he had written that language is "the parent, and not the child of thought" [*I* 132]), although keeping it within a predictable set of 'realistic' human concerns.

Not that *The Importance of Being Earnest* is without magic. A character who never existed is brought back to life when someone claims his name; characters come up with pasts for one another by pointing to a diary, register, and handbag. But all of this is understood by an audience whose response takes the form of rational amusement, not simply over the supposed ubiquitousness of language, but over the characters' earnest relation to it. In order for the play to amuse, the absolute earnestness of the characters' prattle must be taken for granted. For although each character is an assemblage of words, each possesses an *intention*: the intention to marry. Wilde returns playfully to the biological origins of the comic genre in this most cerebral of plays. In the Anthony Asquith film version of the play, for example, Michael Redgrave plays Jack as someone wholly earnest and in love, who can barely hold a teacup without dropping it when in the presence of his beloved. Irony, wit, cynicism are qualities strangely external to the characters in this performance, who are wholly unconscious of what they are saying. When Cecily is about to meet the man she thinks is her scapegrace cousin, she says: "I have never met any really wicked person before. I feel rather frightened. I am so afraid he will look just like everyone else." And after she meets him she says indignantly: "I hope you have not been leading a double life, pretending to be wicked and being really good all the time. That would be hypocrisy."[28] The humor is not simply in what she is saying but in her absolute earnestness toward the man with whom she has already fallen in love. Our emotions, as an audience, are thus engaged not by our sense of the characters' innocence but by their charm. By conventional standards, they are all, every one of them, corrupt. But Wilde's aim is to suggest that not all *standards* are serious.

The only thing that could date *The Importance of Being Earnest*, then, would be if directors ceased to take the characters seriously and misdirected the actors to perform with knowing wit and cynicism. This happens from time to time in revivals that fail because of their insipidity. The humor of the play depends upon the characters' absolutely terrifying dependence on the power of language and naming. As in Charlie Chaplin's performances, we must fear for the comic figure in order to be amused by him, and to fear for him we must trust his intentions. The tension in this sort of comedy, which resembles that accompanying the acrobatic paradoxes of "The Decay of Lying," is something that we must bear, as we watch, for example, Chaplin roller-skate on the edge of a precipice. In the *Laws*, Plato said that we must learn to bear pleasure as well as pain, and those who dislike *The Importance of Being Earnest* (like George Bernard Shaw and Mary McCarthy, who found it to be cold-hearted) are perhaps unprepared to do this. It was Wilde's contention that in his century people as a rule were far more prepared to bear pain than pleasure, and found the former far easier to do. Each generation has its revival of *The Importance of Being Earnest* to remind us of this task. Because of its perpetual challenge, the play is still ahead of its time. Wilde knew he was playing with fire when he wrote it: "How I used to toy with that tiger Life!"[29] he wrote to Reginald Turner, possibly alluding to the homosexual subtext of the action: the secret life of "bunburying." Having passed through the purifying fires of the earlier plays in which a Christian aesthetic of pain is exorcised, Wilde, who literally had to bear his pleasures, understood that pleasure is as realizable as pain. To bear pleasure—that is, to suffer it as well as to give it birth—is what the play is about, a burden that has everything to do with language.

For Algernon and Jack do not move forward in time toward death, but backward in time toward their own christening, to the paradisiac moment of naming. After this creative moment, after the fall into language, all else becomes empty "prattle," in the profound sense in which Kierkegaard uses the word. That *The Importance of Being Earnest* is composed of such prattle is what disturbed Mary McCarthy, who compared it to the suffocating world of Jean-Paul Sartre's *No Exit*. Yet within that idle world of prattle Algernon and Jack work surprisingly hard toward freeing themselves of it by returning to the original word, which, ironically enough, is *earnest* (or Ernest).

The abrupt conclusion of the action, in which the pun on "being Ernest" is loudly proclaimed and the play seems to disappear into the sky like a balloon whose string has been cut, intensifies our feeling that the play's language is a labyrinth in which the characters are forever doomed to wander and play, utterly separate from the circumstantial world in which we ourselves live. This lightness is an essential element in Wilde's theory of art in general; and, as Adorno suggests, it holds for art as a whole, even works preoccupied with the horrors of reality: "Even in Beckett's plays the curtain rises the way it rises on the room with the Christmas presents."[30] But *The Importance of Being Earnest* is unique—"a genre in itself," as critics have recognized[31]—in its delight in the fact of its own existence, that it is art at all. It was in the period of its composition that Wilde's utopianism in fact peaked. On holiday in Algiers shortly before the first trial, he had remarked to Gide, "The sun is jealous of art."[32]

Bringing the Question to Trial

Contradiction experienced to the very depths of
the being tears us heart and soul: It is the cross.
     —Simone Weil, *Gravity and Grace*

WHEN GIDE expressed astonishment at Wilde's being in Algiers at such a precarious time, Wilde made a characteristically equivocal and highly veiled reply. He did not say that he was running away from his life or his problems exactly, but he said: "I am running away from art. I want to worship only the sun. Have you noticed how the sun despises all thought, makes it retreat, take refuge in the shadows. Once thought lived in Egypt; the sun conquered Egypt. It lived for long in Greece; the sun conquered Greece. Then Italy, and then France. Today all thought is pushed back to Norway and Russia, where the sun never comes. The sun is jealous of art."[33] Aside from the inescapably artistic character of this whimsical renunciation of art, it is to be noted that the thought here performs a subtle turnabout (reminiscent of Donne's "The Sun Rising"), for at the end of the passage art has regained a place of honor, displacing "the sun" in importance. The idea that in engaging in litigation against the Marquess of Queensbury, in inviting retribution for his crimes, he was "running away from art," or from the sense of freedom it gave him, is in fact given the lie when, in *De Profundis*, Wilde admits to having experienced a need to explore "the other half of the garden": "There was no pleasure I did not experience. . . . But to have continued the same life would have been wrong because it would have been limiting. I had to pass on. The other half of garden had its secrets for me also." Wilde suggests that this impulse—once again attuned to "secrecy"—was itself an artistic one, a movement simultaneously away from "limitation" and toward formal symmetry, and he goes on to illustrate how it fits into the overall pattern of his work: "all this is foreshadowed and prefigured in my art" (203).

It is no accident, therefore, that one who alludes with such abandon to the paradoxical nature of truth should have engaged in a libel action, which is all about written "truth," and charged someone for writing something that was, in actual fact, true. In *De Profundis* as elsewhere, Wilde fixes on the transformation worked on "truth" when a text changes hands; his lament in what follows, as Edward Said suggests, "is that a text has too much, not too little, circumstantial reality."[34] An affectionate experiment in literary allusion is transformed to the legal liability of print:

> You send me a very nice poem, of the undergraduate school of verse, for my approval: I reply by a letter of fantastic literary conceits. . . . Look at the history of that letter! It passes from you into the hands of a loathesome companion: from him to a gang of black-mailers: copies of it are sent about London to my friends, and to the manager of the theater where my work is being performed: every construction but the right one is put on it: Society is thrilled with the absurd rumours that I have had to pay a huge sum of money for having written an infamous letter to you: this forms the basis of your father's worst attack: I produce the original letter myself in Court to show what it really is: it is denounced by your fa-

ther's counsel as a revolting and insidious attempt to corrupt Innocence:
ultimately it forms part of a criminal charge: the Crown takes it up: the
Judge sums up on it with little learning and much morality: I go to prison
for it at last. That is the result of writing you a charming letter. (*DP*
169–70)

Wilde's abhorrence at being labeled, at having the wealth of his language and his temperament reduced to such paltry material, is no
doubt one reason he became involved in the libel suit in the first
place. When Queensbury labeled him a "somdomite [sic]," the
Marquess was guilty of misrepresenting Wilde's overall character in
every sense *except* the legal. "From a label there is no escape!" cries
Lord Henry in *The Picture of Dorian Gray.* "I refuse the title" (314).

From the essays and dialogues in *Intentions* onward, Wilde
shows himself to be conscious of the Kantian problem of the relative or relational nature of truth. But in the development of his aestheticism, as discussed in the first part of this chapter, Wilde does
not by any means master this problem. Trapped as he is in the inevitable contradiction of the "true" lie—in which "truth" both
refers to the standard of correctness and expresses an imperative of
vitality—he can only allude to the contradiction the way a prisoner,
when given paper to draw on, might draw a picture of his cell without the bars showing. In "The Decay of Lying," for example, Wilde
cannot positively state that what he, in the guise of Vivian, is saying
about art and life is "true" because this would contradict what he
knows to be the contradictory character of truth: the truth of lies
and the lie of truths. The dialogue form, as Wilde is using it here,
suggests that *truth itself is contradictoriness*, or perhaps twofoldness.
Neither can Wilde state *this* truth because to do so would implicitly
cancel the contradictory status of the signified. (Nevertheless, to
posit the truth as *contradictoriness* is not necessarily to utter a contradiction.) From "The Decay of Lying" onward, Wilde is at an impasse on this question.

Whereas Nietzsche stood "in holy dread" before the problem of
"the discordance of art and truth," Wilde persists in roller-skating
near the precipice as happily and serenely as Charlie Chaplin. As an
artist, absorbed in presenting all sides of the question, Wilde de-
lighted in articulating the precariousness of his position and in disarming us; perhaps he disarmed himself. His philosophical vulnerability on the question of truth may in fact have been the crucial

motivating factor in the initiation of a libel suit. He had taken the problem of truth as far as he could take it in his art. Was he then prey to the attraction of another theater, that of the courtroom, to take it further? The one place, perhaps, in which language is weighed as carefully as it is in literature is the court of law. Did Wilde consciously and unconsciously seek this new arena in which to test it?

There is an ambiguous moment during the first trial when Wilde is on the stand. Edward Carson, counsel for the crown, reads one of Wilde's more scandalous aphorisms out loud, then asks: "You think that true?"

> *Wilde.* "I rarely think that anything I write is true."
> *Carson.* "Did you say 'rarely'?"
> *Wilde.* "I said 'rarely.' I might have said 'never'—not true in the actual sense of the word."[35]

Carson almost succeeds in trapping Wilde when he gets him to admit that he "rarely" tells the truth in his writing. If Wilde had stood by the word *rarely*, Carson then could have backed Wilde against the wall with questions like: "*How* rarely? Under what conditions? Is *The Picture of Dorian Gray* true? Are you speaking the truth now?" and, most effectively, "Are these love letters true?" (Wilde had disavowed the personal reference of one by claiming it as a prose poem.) But Wilde sees this coming and so he changes his answer by claiming that he really meant " 'never'—not true in the actual sense of the word." Under these verbal conditions, nothing Wilde wrote—whether aphorisms, novel, or love letter—can be taken literally and used against him. They are examples of "art."

But Wilde's first answer is the honest one, implying that, although what he writes may not always be true ("in the actual sense of the word"—that is, presumably, in the pragmatic sense recognized by a court of law), it may *sometimes* be true (in either "the actual sense" or other senses). Wilde is unwilling absolutely to renounce the relation between art and truth, but neither is he willing to affirm any simple concept of referentiality. The ambiguity suggests, once again, a fundamental equivocation in Wilde, and indeed in nineteenth-century culture generally, one that does not begin to find a resolution until *De Profundis*. The courtroom was Wilde's nemesis on this question. To one who had pledged to live his life as a work of art, there may have been no other way to bring the question to a crisis.

This interpretation of the events displaces the widely accepted, fundamentally sentimental view of Wilde's catastrophe, according to which *it could have been avoided*. Like Cardinal Newman, whom Wilde greatly admired, and who went over to Rome for the sake of sheer intellectual consistency, giving up almost all that he enjoyed in his daily life for what seemed to many to be little more than a theological technicality, Wilde had a "will to truth." Such a will may be partly unconscious, but I have been wary of using the words "conscious" and "unconscious," at least as mutually exclusive terms, preferring to maintain an emphasis on Wilde's whole being, his artistic being. The experimental and effectively self-destructive element in Wilde's conduct may be seen as one aspect of a greater artistic intention or "intellectual conscience," in Nietzsche's words. Wilde himself suggests as much in *De Profundis*. "Nothing really at any period of my life was ever of the smallest importance to me compared with Art" (156). As occupied as Wilde is with understanding how he could have let Douglas's problems infect his own life, his interest in the experience as a whole is largely compositional: "In all that I have said I am simply concerned with my own mental attitude towards *life as a whole*" (*DP* 199, emphasis added).

Resolution in *De Profundis*

For this reason *De Profundis*, as personal an utterance as it may appear, is best understood as a culmination of Wilde's philosophic exploration of the vexed relation of art and truth. It may well be, as Ellmann concludes, that the work is one of the greatest love letters ever written, but it is restrictive to see it primarily as a love letter. Ellmann condescends to Wilde when he dismisses the extended discussion of the figure of Christ—not something normally associated with the genre of the love letter—as self-serving. Surely its place in the work is not *merely personal*. We shall see that even the most personal utterances in the letter are part of a larger philosophical pattern of recurrence and overcoming.

In drawing on the life of Jesus, Wilde is gaining distance on his own life at the same time that he is coming nearer to its secret meaning. The meditation shows above all how decisively he was moving away from creating works of art for the world and how consciously he was developing and embracing the idea of self-creation. For what makes the life of Christ relevant to Wilde's experience in prison is not that Christ offers redemption for sins but that he represents the supreme act of "self-development," which, for Wilde, has become the essence of the artistic life.

Though Wilde writes of eternity and the soul, his interest is not in "salvation" in the traditional Christian sense. Hence Wilde's preference for the Fourth Gospel, which he regarded as Gnostic. It is not a matter of deliverance from sin and guilt, as in orthodox patristic Christendom, but of the realization of the spirit in the world. Had Wilde undertaken to attack the church more explicitly in *De Profundis*, his own ideas of salvation and redemption might have been taken more seriously, at least by the relative few who take heterodox ideas seriously. Hilary Fraser's judgment is typical: "One would not wish to make claims for the theological credibility of [Wilde's idea of] Christ as a work of art. [It has] little to do with historical Christianity and [is] decidedly heterodox."[36] Of course Wilde would have agreed with the second statement.[37] In 1909, James Joyce recognized that in *De Profundis* Wilde "kneels before a gnostic Christ": he "closed the book of his spirit's rebellion with an act of spiritual dedication."[38]

Wilde's skepticism toward historical Christianity came from a deeply meditated, cosmopolitan conception of the story of Jesus. He said once to a friend that Christ was not divine: " 'It would place too broad a gulf between him and the human soul.' "[39] And he refused to admit that there had been any true Christians since the first: "There were Christians before Christ.... The unfortunate thing is that there have been none since" (*DP* 215). Nietzsche writes in precisely this vein: "There was only *one* Christian, and he died on the cross" (*A* 612). Of course Wilde, being Wilde, must make one exception; he does so in St. Francis of Assisi. Once out of prison, however, he would remark: "Like dear St Francis of Assisi I am wedded to Poverty: but in my case the marriage is not a success."[40] Wilde did not think of himself as a Christian in an orthodox sense at any point in his adult life, least of all when he was in prison, where he was so far away from his goal of "the frank acceptance of everything" and so conscious of the neglect of organized, Christian society. But in *De Profundis* Wilde distinguishes a true Christianity, as allied with art, from "the church," and he therefore understands

Christianity in a new way. His meditation on Christianity shows the powerful influence of Renan and, as I shall indicate, comes compellingly near to Nietzsche's view of Christ in *The Antichrist*. As one who was "the first to conceive the divided races as a unity" (*DP* 205), Jesus was implicitly cosmopolitan—Nietzsche calls him "this great cosmopolitan" (*A* 585)—someone who counters or overcomes the various tribal, organizational, and nationalist structures that prevent any real acknowledgement of what links us to the outcasts, the criminals, the poor, the other races. Christ "gave to man an extended, a Titan personality. Since his coming, the history of each separate individual is, or can be made, the history of the world" (*DP* 208),[41] just as in Kant the individual forms the basis of an "idea of universal history with a cosmopolitan intent." Kant writes that "what strikes us as complicated and unpredictable in the single individual may in the history of the entire species be discovered to be the steady progress and slow development of its original capacities."[42]

The idea of reception that had earlier figured in Wilde's attempt to resolve the quandary of an art that is in the world but not of it, an art capable of death and resurrection, finds its full development here. At the beginning of his meditation, Wilde pauses to distinguish himself from Pater, who, like Wilde, sought to "reconcile the artistic life with the life of religion." Pater, he implies, placed an exaggerated emphasis on spectatorship, giving insufficient attention to the idea of self-development. Marius is "a spectator merely," he writes, "and perhaps a little too much occupied with the comeliness of the vessels of the Sanctuary to notice that it is the Sanctuary of Sorrow that he is gazing at" (*DP* 204). Wilde suggests by this image that, like the travelers to Emmaus, whom he alludes to later, Marius looks without seeing and listens without hearing. Wilde writes that Christ is "like a work of art himself. He does not really teach one anything, but by being brought into his presence one becomes something. And everybody is predestined to his presence. Once at least in his life each man walks with Christ to Emmaus" (215–16). The static separation between art and life, subject and object, art and truth, is overcome here by means of an idea of *becoming*, or of what Baudelaire calls "transformation." If the work of art is to be understood, Baudelaire writes in 1855 in a discussion of cosmopolitan criticism, "the critic, the viewer, must bring about within himself a transformation, which is something of a mystery."[43] Wilde writes: "the contemplative life, the life that has for its aim not *doing* but *being*, and not being merely, but *becoming*—that is what the critical spirit can give us" (*I* 182).

With this Baudelairean emphasis upon the *effects* of art, Wilde illuminates the distinction, not between art and life, but between art and didacticism. The work of art, whether in the form of a person, painting, or poem, does not "teach one anything, but by being brought into [its] presence one becomes something." It is this essential transformation, this transformation of essence, this giving oneself to the text in order to find oneself, that Wilde propounds in *De Profundis* as a whole. The issue is epitomized in his pronouncement that, as in Art one is concerned with what a particular thing is to oneself at a particular moment, "so it is also in the ethical evolution of one's character" (197). It is not "what one does" that signifies but "what one becomes" (196).

The aesthetic state in Wilde, or more precisely the state of aesthetic reception, is not one in which the mind is merely a *tabula rasa* that registers without any selection or refraction. As is made clear in "The Critic as Artist," the aesthetically receptive critic, rather than passive, has a particular *temperament*, one that is not dominated by reason but itself *shapes*. (Baudelaire calls this "a phenomenon of will-power acting on his imagination."[44]) In Wilde, as in Kant (who emphasizes the faculty of "building" or *Bilden*), there is no consciousness of any kind that is purely passive. But neither is the mind simply assertive, arbitrarily imposing its modes of perception onto the object. These modes are suspended in true creation, as Schiller keeps suggesting in the *Aesthetic Letters*. In the aesthetic state, one is essentially vibrating between activity and passivity; the antitheses as such are suspended. One becomes. One receives *in order to* become; one does not receive in order to consume or simply to mirror.

The Christ, therefore, does not have anything to teach us in the formal sense understood by the Pharisees, nor is he out to save us in the traditional sense of the church. Merely to "believe," to repent, to count on "the redeemer" somehow to salvage one by his example—all of this is superfluous in both Wilde's and Nietzsche's understanding of the figure of Jesus. "I need not tell you that to me Reformations in Morals are as meaningless and vulgar as Reformations in Theology," declares Wilde (*DP* 217). Like his younger contemporary, Nietzsche writes of Christ's "deep instinct for how one must *live*, in order to feel oneself 'in heaven,' to feel 'eternal,' while in all other behavior one decidedly does *not* feel oneself 'in heaven'— this alone is the psychological reality of 'redemption.' A new way of life, *not* a new faith" (*A* 607). In both Wilde and Nietzsche, "redemption" is not denied but reinterpreted, as is the idea of an *imitatio Christi*. The kingdom of heaven is not a future residence or possession but, in both thinkers, an "experience of the heart" (*A* 608). Wilde writes of that which is within or "in the midst" of us: "If I may not find its secret within myself, I shall never find it. If I have not got it already, it will never come to me" (197). Christ cannot "teach" the secret of living then, because, in the words of Nietzsche, "it *lives*, it resists all formulas" (*A* 605). Organized religion actually makes for the opposite of the *practice* that is Christ's real "legacy to mankind" (*A* 609). Those who worship at the altar or bow before the priest, as Wilde says, may be capable of receiving this knowledge only in spite of their religion and not because of it. As Wilde had earlier suggested in "The Soul of Man under Socialism," the concept of the church is precisely what Jesus attacks; in Nietzsche's words, he puts it "*beneath* and *behind* himself*" (*A* 609).

*R*eformations that are based on obedience to some external precept are meaningless because the *trans*formation must come from within. In *The Antichrist*, Nietzsche emphasizes this inwardness in his image of Christ as one who "spun the world out of himself" (585). In *De Profundis*, Wilde remarks upon the inward nature of his task again and again: "Everything must come to one out of one's own nature" (177). "I have to get it all out of myself" (196). "I must get far more out of myself than ever I got, and ask far less of the world than ever I asked." Wilde becomes laceratingly conscious of the fact that "my ruin came not from too great individualism of life, but from too little. The one disgraceful, unpardonable, and to all time contemptible action of my life was my allowing myself to be forced into appealing to Society for help and protection" (219–20).

In spite of Nietzsche's attack on the morbid and inauthentic character of historical Christianity, he writes that there is an authentic Christianity, which is a possible *practice*. "Such a life is still possible today, for certain people even necesssary: genuine, original Christianity will be possible at all times. . . . Not a faith but a doing; above all, a *not* doing of many things, another state of *being*" (*A* 613). In prison, Wilde became one of those for whom this sort of

Christianity, as a state of being, became "necessary." With everything taken from him, he had no choice but to renounce it all—precisely in order to "accept" what had happened. Having lost his good name, his social position, his former happiness, his freedom and his wealth, he must even suffer the loss of his children, who are taken from him by the law. "It was a blow so appalling that I did not know what to do. . . . I saw then that the only thing for me was to accept everything" (207).

Yet the acceptance of everything does not take place as a single act; it is part of an extended process. Just as Nietzsche's meditation on Jesus unfolds at the exact center of *The Antichrist*, surrounded on either side by diatribes against the "vampirism" of orthodox Christendom, Wilde's meditation on the meaning of Jesus's life as it relates to his own comes in the middle of *De Profundis*, and is surrounded on either side by lengthy denunciations of Douglas. The argument of *De Profundis* develops across three distinct sections: in the first, Wilde reviews his relationship with Alfred Douglas up to the time of his imprisonment. Full of resentment and recrimination, this section culminates in the recognition that he must forgive Douglas, not for Douglas's sake but for his own. Wilde's conscious attempt to take responsibility for what has happened comprises the second part. It begins with a summary of all that he was and all he had accomplished before the initiation of the legal action. The difficulty in accepting what has happened leads Wilde to meditate the life of one who *was* able to accept everything. Thus follows the nucleus of the second part: the meditation on Jesus as an artist, whose life was itself a work of art. Wilde's acknowledgment of how far he himself really is from absolute acceptance makes him return, in the third section, to self-recrimination and attacks on Douglas. But at the final "moment" of the letter, Wilde imagines release from the morass of bitterness once again: "Time and space, succession and extension, are merely accidental conditions of thought. The Imagination can transcend them, and move in a free sphere of ideal existences" (239). On the other hand, as Wilde puts it earlier in the letter, "One can realise a thing in a single moment, but one loses it in the long hours that follow with leaden feet. It is so difficult to keep 'heights that the soul is competent to gain.' We think in Eternity, but we move slowly through Time" (202–3).

This continuing pattern of descent into the temporal world and momentary ascent from out of its midst, of alternate rejection and acceptance of his fate, is what gives the narrative of *De Profundis* its powerful surging rhythm. For the struggle we see taking place before our eyes in *De Profundis*—and what makes it so moving despite and because of the presence of all of its "verbal decorations," as Yeats called them, all of its immersion in the smallest details of a degrading intimacy—is the struggle of a soul to will the recurrence of a life down to the last repellent detail in order to affirm it, to achieve a state of mind in which he would prefer nothing more passionately than the repetition of that life just as it has been, in which he would come to see that all events of his past, even events of irreparable horror and desolation, were "for the best," a state of mind which could turn the most questionable things to one's advantage and make one stronger; in short, what Nietzsche calls *amor fati*, love of fate: "my formula for greatness in a human being is *amor fati*: that one wants nothing to be different, not forward, not backward, not in all eternity. Not merely bear what is necessary, still less conceal it . . . but *love* it" (*EH* 258).

Wilde understands the magnitude of his task:

> I need not say that my task does not end there [with learning compassion]. . . . Neither Religion, Morality, nor Reason can help me at all. . . . [I]t must be nothing external to me. Its symbols must be of my own creating. Only that is spiritual which makes its own form. . . . The important thing, the thing that lies before me, the thing that I have to do . . . is to absorb into my nature all that has been done to me, to make it part of me, to accept it without complaint, fear, or reluctance. The supreme vice is shallowness. Whatever is realised is right. . . .
>
> To reject one's own experience is to arrest one's own development. To deny one's own experience is to put a lie into the lips of one's own life. It is no less than a denial of the Soul. For just as the body absorbs things of all kinds, things common and unclean no less than those that the priest or a vision has cleansed, and converts them into swiftness or strength . . . so the Soul in its turn has its nutritive functions also, and can transform into noble moods of thought, and passions of high import, what in itself is base, cruel, and degrading: nay, more, may find in these its most august modes of assertion, and can often reveal itself most perfectly through what was intended to desecrate or destroy. (*PF* 196–98)

For both Wilde and Nietzsche, there is no divine providence at work in the world. It is up to us instead to engender the actuality of a "Personal Providence" (*JW* 213), something that calls for cultivated skill in interpreting and negotiating events, an artistic skill.

Throughout *De Profundis* Wilde draws our attention to the artistic techniques he is using to make sense of his life, particularly the techniques of foregrounding and distancing. As Nietzsche had urged one to do a decade earlier, Wilde achieves an "artistic remoteness" from himself (*JW* 146). In describing a minor incident that took place while he was in prison—Douglas had tactlessly written in a message: "Prince Fleur de Lys wishes to be remembered to you"—Wilde concludes: "The great things in life are what they seem to be, and for that reason, strange as it may sound to you, are often difficult to interpret. But the little things of life are symbols. . . . Your seemingly casual choice of a feigned name was, and will remain, symbolic. It reveals you" (183). In *De Profundis*, as in the story of Christ, the "little things of life" are foregrounded because of their symbolic or parabolic content.

Wilde recomposes his life in memory, re-collecting it; he comes to perceive events that heretofore had seemed irredeemably failed and repugnant as necessary to its artistic unity:

> I don't regret for a single moment having lived for pleasure. I did it to the full, as one should do everything that one does to the full. There was no pleasure I did not experience. . . . But to have continued the same life would have been wrong because it would have been limiting. I had to pass on. The other half of the garden had its secrets for me also. . . . Of course all this is foreshadowed and prefigured in my art. . . . [In] the prose-poem of the man who from the bronze of the image of the "Pleasure that liveth for a Moment" has to make the image of the "Sorrow that abideth for Ever" it is incarnate. It could not have been otherwise. At every single moment of one's life one is what one is going to be no less than what one has been. Art is a symbol, because man is a symbol. (203–4)

The passage begins by affirming the pleasure and joy of his life, then affirming its proximity, in fact its *integral* relation, to the pain. One cannot say Yes to the pleasure without saying Yes to everything. The works he has written are themselves confirmation of this. "Did you ever say Yes to one joy?" Nietzsche asks in *Zarathustra*, "O my friends, then you said Yes to *all* the woe. All things are chained and entwined together . . . if ever you wanted one moment twice, if ever you said, 'You please me, happiness, instant, moment!' then you wanted everything to return!" (*Z* 331–32). To love one's fate is to realize the ultimate interconnectedness of all things, the inconspicuous logic by which the most difficult, harmful and questionable of experiences do not detract from but *complete* the whole. The "thing that I have to do, or be for the brief remainder of my days one maimed, marred, and *incomplete*," writes Wilde, "is to absorb into my nature all that has been done to me" (197, emphasis added). With this retrieved personal redemption, his life becomes a "prophecy," a "realisation of some ideal"; the past and the future can come together in a "completed" work, constituting what Wilde calls (no doubt invoking the etymology of the word) a "symbol." Each moment resonates in a temporal fabric of past and future moments; "Art is a symbol, because man is a symbol."

Sorrow has everything to do with this process of symbolization, in which the past entails a promise of the future:

> My friendship with you . . . appears to me always as a prelude consonant with those varying modes of anguish which each day I have to realise; nay, more, to necessitate them even; as though my life, whatever it had seemed to myself and others, had all the while been a real Symphony of Sorrow, passing through its rhythmically linked movements to its certain resolution, with that *inevitableness* that in Art characterises the treatment of every great theme. . . . [The] *remembrance* of suffering in the past is necessary to us as the *warrant*, the evidence, of our continued identity. (164–65, emphasis added)

"Imagination is always melancholy,"[45] Kierkegaard suggests, perhaps because of this *inevitableness*, characteristic of both art and the fully realized life.[46] Because sorrow is a mode of existence in which the outward is identified with the inward—"Behind Joy and Laughter there may be a temperament, coarse, hard and callous. But behind Sorrow there is always Sorrow"—it is not only "the type and *test* of all great art" (201),[47] but the warrant, in its very irreducibility, of our continued identity. Music, which to Wilde always represented the ineffability of art, is the perfect metaphor for what he is saying. The "remembrance of suffering in the past," which is likened to the experience of listening to a piece of music, "passing through its rhythmically linked movements to its certain resolution," has become the very condition for shaping his life into art. His life, like that of Jesus, has been "tested" by sorrow and thus can be forged into a work of art, that is, a symbol in which life and art are finally one.

In the central section of *De Profundis*, Wilde makes us feel that he *almost* succeeds in achieving, not reformation, conversion, or forgiveness, but the other "state of being," the "frank acceptance of all experiences" that is "the true life of the artist" (204). He repeatedly emphasizes the difficulty of the struggle in phrasing such as: "I am quite ready [to say that I have ruined myself]. I am trying to do so" (194); "I have got to make . . . these things just and right to me;" "I want to get to the point" (197), and so on. But the mood shifts. He again feels his humiliation, how repellent and demeaning every aspect of his tragedy has been, down to the clownlike prison clothes he must wear. His thoughts turn back to Douglas and to loathsome memories of their life together—including the constant fever of angry telegrams and letters, the tedious visits to lawyers, the money spent on every useless extravagance, the miseries of bankruptcy; he moves then to the demand that Douglas himself realize what has happened and, at the last, he summons the faith that Douglas will. Wilde never doubts that Douglas loves him or that he will answer the letter (as in fact Douglas did). Wilde concludes with the statement on time quoted earlier, the aim of which is to inspire in Douglas the "true temper of soul" that he has tried so hard to realize in himself.

In *De Profundis* Wilde has moved beyond what Nietzsche describes as the "profound superficiality" of the Apollonian stance, beyond the world with which Wilde is sometimes associated. His earlier love of surface, exaggerated worship of pure form, refusal of pessimism, delight in what is illusory, deliquescent, and masked— these have receded before the more direct, but no less artistic, confrontation with suffering that takes place in *De Profundis*. Whereas in the comparatively flat Apollonian perspective one willfully becomes what one is not, *amor fati* makes it possible, through entry into a new dynamically interwoven temporality, to "become what one is." At the end of *De Profundis*, Wilde writes, "What lies before me is my past. I have got to make myself look on that with different eyes. . . . This I cannot do by ignoring it, or slighting it, or praising it, or denying it. It is only to be done by fully accepting it as an inevitable part of the evolution of my life and character" (239). *What lies before me is my past*: past, present, and future are the "conditions of thought," as Wilde states at the beginning of this passage, conditions which the imagination can effectively transcend (as it transcends the data of perception). Yet to transcend is to descend; as in the earlier meditation on Christ as a work of art, Wilde once again realizes that for everything to be overcome, everything must be accepted. *What lies before me is my past*. The whole thing must be gone over again, because the whole thing is eternally before him, eternally in question.

The exalted state of mind in which *De Profundis* was composed, and in which imaginative freedom is linked inextricably to the necessity of "accepting everything," did not entirely dissipate in the period following his release from prison. Ellmann puts the accent on Wilde's decline during this period, but—quite apart from the production of *The Ballad of Reading Gaol*, a poem which had a popular and critical success, and which Ellmann himself considers unforgettable—there is evidence of a certain crystallization in Wilde's attitude toward language. This is not a matter of any systematic theoretic elaboration, of course, but of a feeling and a mood, what the Germans would call *Befindlichkeit*. And it is something that can only be hinted. In a letter of 1897 to Frank Harris, he writes, "Words, *now*, to me signify things, actualities, real emotions, realised thoughts. . . . I am grateful for a thousand things, from my good friends down to the sun and the sea. But I cannot say more than that I am grateful. I cannot make phrases about it."[48] It would seem that Wilde, in the name of a certain gratitude, had come now entirely to identify with the spirit of language "in itself"; its virtuality was his actuality, just as for Novalis the relations between things are secretly mirrored in the "tender workings" of language.[49] He had experienced inwardly, or rather with a new overwhelming concreteness, the truth of his earlier proposition that language is "the parent, and not the child, of thought."

Although this relatively modest and indeed fragmentary realization of the immanence of language may have made it possible for Wilde more fully or more purely to accept the painfulness of his circumstances after his release from prison, it naturally could not alter those circumstances or heal the external rift with the world. In prison he had written: "Between my art and the world there is now a wide gulf, but between my Art and myself there is none. I hope at least there is none" (*DP* 218). As the last sentence implies, and as Ellmann amply documents, the struggle to sustain an artistic identity continued in spite of the intimations concerning language. From Berneval-sur-Mer, he wrote to Ross, "This is my first day alone, and of course a very unhappy one. I begin to realise my terrible position of isolation, and I have been rebellious and bitter of heart all day."[50] Note the fatalistic "of course" in the first sentence, together with the almost Miltonic grandeur of phrase in the second. It was in such phrases, he is suggesting, that any true redemption is to be found. Scorning any note of pity or of self-pity right through to the end, Wilde could summon up nobility in the most humiliating of circumstances. A few months before his death, he encountered in Paris an old friend of his mother's, Comtesse Anna de Brémont, who had felt it necessary to cut him at a cafe, only, to her relief, to run into him the next day on a passenger steamer on the Seine. Characteristically, he admonishes her: " 'Life held to my lips a full flavoured cup and I drank it to the dregs . . . Contessa, don't sorrow for me.' "[51]

♫ Epilogue: Cosmopolitan Melancholy

> For imagination is always melancholy.
> —Kierkegaard, *Either/Or*

NOTHING SEEMS to make Oscar Wilde more remote from us than his reputation as a storyteller. "Wilde did not converse," wrote Gide, "He narrated."[1] From Yeats's perspective, "he seemed . . . a figure from another age, an audacious, Italian fifteenth-century fig-ure." His talk was "completely unreproducible," wrote another ob-server, so enmeshed was it in "gesture and voice" and in his own de-light in delivery. Yeats recorded his "astonishment" on first hearing Wilde: "I never before heard a man talking with sentences, as if he had written them all overnight with labour and yet all sponta-neous."[2] Wilde's fame in the mid-1880s was due only in part to Gilbert and Sullivan's satire of the aesthete in *Patience*. The most acute observers recognized at once the last of a disappearing type: a "figure from another age." Wilde announced in his person what Walter Benjamin would suggest a generation later in his criticism, that the figure of the storyteller was vanishing, and that the art of storytelling was coming to an end: "Less and less frequently do we encounter people with the ability to tell a tale properly. More and more often there is embarrassment all around when the wish to hear a story is expressed. It is as if something that seemed inalien-able to us, the securest among our possessions, were taken from us: the ability to exchange experiences."[3] Wilde's fairy tales, published in 1888 and 1891, mark his effort to restore the art of storytelling to his generation. In the process of writing them down, he seems to have made an admission of failure in recognizing that experience cannot be exchanged. This is the theme of the penultimate story, "The Devoted Friend," in which the listener of a moral tale is shown to be impervious to its meaning, and it is pursued in the final tale of narcissistic self-destruction, "The Remarkable Rocket."

As if conceding that his art had reached an impasse that could only be overcome by an advance in critical thought (an idea that it-self would find expression in "The Critic as Artist"), Wilde turned his attention to criticism and, in January of 1889, published "The Decay of Lying." There, on a critical-philosophical level, he takes up the question of an atrophy of experience and, as I suggested ear-lier, he anticipates many of the insights of Benjamin's "The Story-teller." The overall problem that both Wilde and Benjamin address in these works concerns the diminishing place of "art" in human "life," or in a society in which useful information predominates over all other forms of meaning. The examination of Wilde's life in pre-ceding chapters leaves us with the same predicament: the threat-ened position of the artist in modern society. When Wilde says in prison that "if life be, as it surely is, a problem to me, I am no less a problem to life," he refers not only to the disjunction between this "poor, probable, uninteresting human life" (*I* 30)—that is, the ethi-cal character of life in utilitarian society—and the aesthetic poten-tial in each of us; he refers as well to the fact that he himself as an artist had been scorned by the community.

In Wilde's evolving multilateral project, we find these tensions between the aesthetic and the ethical taken to an extreme and ig-nited; the idea of a cosmopolitan criticism is what survives the blast. This is not to say that, for art to survive in the modern world, Wilde believed that it must become criticism, although he certainly wanted his audience to be aware of the relation between the excess of bad "creative" work being published and the relatively small quantity of excellent criticism.[4] He meant rather that the true work of art, which is simultaneously more self-sufficient and more pro-tean than any commodity of industrial society, will survive if and only if a cosmopolitan criticism comes into being. As a form of con-templation at once moral and aesthetic, such criticism has no direct bearing on the opinions or prejudices of existing societies or even of the critic himself, who as it were brackets these things in order to receive what the work of art has to reveal that is new. All such im-mediately interested concepts are not denied but suspended. To those who would insist that it is impossible, in even a provisional way, to rise above one's prejudices, or to suspend the presupposi-tions of class, ethnicity, and the like, Wilde would have only one answer: such persons should not be writing criticism. They lack the proper temperament for it, he would argue, one distinguished above all by its power of distance, which is to say, its creative *receptivity* to new forms and impressions.[5] Many critics writing today would of course disagree with Wilde; an entire school of literary criticism has grown up on the principle of the reader's self-assertion. To Wilde, such active intervention bespeaks the audience's efforts to dominate the work of art. The reluctance of much recent American criticism to immerse itself in the text it treats is a symptom of this strident subjectivism. To use a metaphor that Benjamin applies to the bourgeoisie, many American critics today become so short of breath when above the threshold of national interest, of popular culture, of race or "gender," that they can form no conception at all of issues on a world-historical scale. What prevents them from doing so is not ignorance of either the world or history, but a certain indifference to what has traditionally gone under the name of art, or, more precisely, a refusal to privilege the concept of art. This takes the form of a refusal to *distinguish* art from the sphere of ethics in a practical sense—that is, in the sense in which ethics may be said to encompass all action and politics. Whereas Wilde insisted that the connection between the ethical and the aesthetic can only be understood if one maintains a practical distinction between them, recent critics wish to collapse the distinction altogether by effectively reducing art to politics, or the work of art to the document. Such critics have something in common with the Victorian reviewers who came to art only via a platform of puritanical ethics. Wilde never tired of inveighing against the "pseudo-ethical criticism" of these writers, not because they were puritanical—a fact that only amused him—but because they threatened the integrity of art, or what he called the morality of art: its capacity to forward ethical discovery by virtue of its formal aloofness. From the earliest period of his criticism, Wilde insisted that "by keeping aloof from the social problems of the day . . . [art] more completely realises for us that which we desire. For to most of us the real life is the life we do not lead."

Ethics "makes existence possible" whereas aesthetics gives it "progress and variety and change." It is the artist who "accepts the facts of life, and yet transforms them" in order to show "their true ethical import." Puritan, preacher, journalist, lawyer, statistician, or scientist: none of these sees, in his instituted one-sidedness, the "true ethical import" of events as the artist sees it, the artist who in Wilde is a critic and historian as much as a poet or musician. Art returns us to ethics and ethics, says Wilde—if it has any bearing on the truth—returns us to art. In this way, ethics and aesthetics achieve the slippery footing they deserve, the sliding sands necessary for their continued vitality and fecundity. On these sliding sands Wilde's entire enterprise was erected. In trying to make his life into a work of art, he conducted an "experiment in living," as Yeats has said, like walking on water.

Sliding sands, slippery footing: these words raise the specter of nihilism, or that condition of mind in which, theoretically at least, "everything is permitted." But there is a difference between a state of mind in which everything is permitted and one in which nothing is denied. The first involves a loosening of prohibitions, an opening wide of all moral framework, an open invitation to rise, sink, drift, what you will. The second is an imperative, the imperative to deny nothing in one's survey of the vast range of human possibilities, a requirement to hold fast in one's thought and vision to the whole. It is this imperative that the speaker of Baudelaire's "Epilogue" invokes as he rises above the city, the "enormous trull," at the same time that he looks deep into its horrors: "Hospital, brothel, prison, and such hells." Only from the "steep height" of the citadel can the experience of "harlots and hunted" be understood.[6] Baudelaire, Wilde, and Benjamin, each fascinated by a supposed connection between prostitution and art, sought in their different ways to know all aspects of the body and mind *denied* by bourgeois civilization.[7]

To Wilde, art is an end in itself because man is an end in himself. The society that fails to recognize this fact but instead treats man as an instrument and as a *means* to an end will treat art in the same way. At the beginning of the nineteenth century, Carlyle took note of the mechanical spirit as the cardinal "sign of the times" and bore witness to the age's declining awareness of "the inward primary powers of man," of man as "creator and producer." At the end of the century, Wilde—a satirist and not a mystic, but no less a prophet than Carlyle—held the same mirror up to the community in the name of human creation, of art. "All art is quite useless," he said (*DG* xi). It is possibly the most ambiguous statement he ever made.[8]

Art is "useless" because, in a pervasively utilitarian society, it *must* be so in order to endure; otherwise it becomes grist for the bourgeois moral order, as the hack reviewers and members of the "police-court of literature" would have it be. If it is to do its work, it must be in some measure out of reach. In its very lightness, in the fact that "it opens out over the reality to whose violence it bears witness," it constitutes a "critique of the brute seriousness that reality imposes on human beings;" its gravity is comprised in its promotion of a "change in the existing consciousness."[9] With satiric bitterness, Wilde is saying to his age: you have *made* art useless by your insistent utilitarianism. Like the auctioneer, you understand the price of everything and the value of nothing. In the end, society did not know how to value Wilde, though it well appreciated his price as a commodity in the journalist trade. "Originality in thought and action, though no one says that it is not a thing to be admired, nearly all, at heart, think that they can do very well without it"—thus John Stuart Mill.[10] Even artists thought Wilde dispensable and refused to join in an effort to mitigate a sentence they knew might kill him. "All art is quite useless," and if art is useless, man is useless. We owe it to Wilde that, in his deeply humane production and by the example of his life, he invited his century to consider this possibility of necessary uselessness, that he brought it to this precipice.

 Notes

Preface

1. By André Gide in 1905 and later by George Bernard Shaw (1918) and Thomas Mann (1959).

2. Trilling, *Sincerity and Authenticity*, 118.

3. At the conclusion of *Oscar Wilde*, Roditi insisted that "Wilde possessed a more conscious philosophy of art" than either the Pre-Raphaelites or Pater, although Roditi focused on the English and literary, rather than cosmopolitan and philosophical, nature of this consciousness (224). Richard Ellmann said of Wilde that "he laid the basis for many critical positions which are still debated in much the same terms, and which we like to attribute to more ponderous names" (Ellmann, introduction to *Artist as Critic*, x).

4. In Germany, however, Wilde's reputation as a thinker has been high for decades (see Fletcher and Stokes, "Oscar Wilde"). For a thorough review of research on Wilde, and of the increasing emphasis on Wilde as a professional writer, see Small's *Oscar Wilde Revalued*.

5. Four recent examples of this scholarship may be found in the work of Dellamora, Dollimore, Dowling (*Hellenism and Homosexuality*), and Schmidgall. Earlier research into the homosexual context of Wilde's life and work—for example, by Nassaar, Weeks, and Stokes ("Wilde at Bay")—provided an important foundation for later studies.

6. For example, Gagnier's *Idylls of the Marketplace* offers a materialist reading of Wilde's works that illuminates his relations to his audiences in full historical detail. Because Gagnier believes that Wilde "can *only* be understood in relation to his audiences and the social institutions in which art forms are developed and distributed" (3, emphasis added), her treatment of both the idealist and idealistic strains in Wilde's thought is necessarily limited. For example, Wilde's theory of cosmopolitan criticism, which Wilde developed out of a complex variety of sources that Gagnier ignores—the Stoics, Kant, Baudelaire, and Arnold—is reduced to the statement "if everyone were a literary critic, no one would make war" (47). In contrast, Freedman's *Professions of Taste* acknowledges the literary as well as the historical

complexity of aestheticism, but without seriously engaging the tradition of aesthetic philosophy, which is of less moment to the author than current concerns within the Anglo-American academy (see xxviii–xxx). At the conclusion of his study, Freedman bids "good riddance" to the "privileging of a fully autonomous aesthetic sphere" but expresses hope that "[its] passing . . . create[s] space for new imaginings. . . . It may well be that the forging of a new idiom to reckon with the experiences of beauty and pleasure is the next challenge that awaits us" (257). In a similar vein, Dollimore acknowledges that his (materialist) reading of Wilde's aesthetic in *Sexual Dissidence* is "avowedly partial" and that "there is of course more to be said . . . about other of [Wilde's] ideas which intersect with and contradict the transgressive aesthetic explored here" (4n). In short, it is not uncommon for these critics to acknowledge the possibility that the question of Wilde's aesthetic is more complex than a strictly materialist reading will allow.

7. Several major contextual studies give Wilde more credit for intellectual independence than the works cited in the preceding note. See, for example, the illuminating discussion of Wilde's attitude, as an artist, to the power and presence of journalism, in the concluding chapter of Stokes's *In the Nineties* (161–66), and Small's penetrating treatment of Wilde's strategic reaction against dominant categories of thought in *Conditions for Criticism* (112–30).

8. Wilde's cosmopolitanism must also be distinguished from what is called *multiculturalism*. The breadth with which the word *cosmopolitanism* is defined in current usage may be seen in many publications (see, for example, "Replies to Nussbaum," a series of responses to Nussbaum's "Patriotism or Cosmopolitanism?"). Although in chapter 2 I discuss the significance of the word in detail, it may be useful here to clarify that by *cosmopolitanism*, Wilde did not mean nomadism, identification with a political abstraction, or, as I have suggested, denial of one's roots. A heightened sense of national character may well be an essential element of the widest cosmopolitanism. (In "The Critic as Artist" Wilde writes that "it is only by contact with the art of foreign nations that the art of a country gains that individual and separate life that we call nationality" [*I* 162].) Recent work in Wilde studies by Small stresses Wilde's close attention to English culture in his formation of a radicalism that is usually associated with France (see "Literary Radicalism"). In chapter 2 I suggest that Wilde worked through the problem of the relation between ethics and aesthetics by reexamining the Victorian prose writers' stalemate on this question. Wilde's contribution to aesthetic philosophy rose from struggles with his own cultural heritage.

9. Pater, *Renaissance*, 1128.

10. Quoted in Ellmann, introduction to *Artist as Critic*, xi.

11. Karl Kraus (1874–1936), Austrian writer, satirist, and as we say now, "performance artist," who lived in Vienna at the turn of the century. "He will pay any price to get himself talked about," writes Benjamin. Benjamin quotes Kraus as describing himself in terms very similar to those in which we would describe Wilde: "I am perhaps the first instance of a writer who simultaneously writes and acts his writing" (*Reflections* 251–52).

12. Benjamin, *Reflections*, 272.

13. Roditi, *Wilde*, 181.

1. Wilde's Play-Drive

1. Schiller, *Aesthetic Education*, 109.

2. See, for example, Jerome Buckley's *Turning Key*: "The prose of *De Profundis* . . . is often implausible, derivative, and self-indulgent" (99). Together with the autobiographies of George Moore and Edmund Gosse, *De Profundis* is of interest to Buckley mainly as an autobiography "moving toward one of its most characteristic twentieth-century forms, the autobiographical novel" (113).

3. See Adorno, *Minima Moralia*, chapter 22, which might show the influence of Wilde.

4. "Gathering all we are into one desperate effort to see and touch, we shall hardly have time to make theories about the things we see and touch," writes Pater in the conclusion to *The Renaissance* (1129), as though this were not itself a theory. For a succinct summary of the major differences between Wilde and Pater, see *ON* 14–17. See also West's discussion of Pater's debt to Schiller: "Pater was propagating the weakness of German idealist philosophy," when he made the goal of life purely aesthetic, unlike Schiller (and, we might add, Wilde), who made it political as well. Pater "abstracts art from activity, aesthetics from politics, the individual from society" (*Mountain in the Sunlight*, 112–14).

5. Small, *Oscar Wilde Revalued*, 3.

6. Le Rouge's reminiscence appeared in *Nouvelles litteraires* of 3 and 10 November 1928 (quoted in Schmidgall, *Stranger Wilde*, 255–56).

7. The editors of *ON* emphasize Wilde's unique "synthesis" of the matter and mind controversies prevailing at Oxford when he was there (34).

8. The sense of fate, which was strong in Wilde from his youth, is one reason Richard Ellmann gives to support his conclusion that Wilde had syphilis, although, as Ellmann admits, "the evidence is not decisive" (*OW* 92–93). I suggest that Wilde's sense of fate may have originated in an understanding of the formal "inevitability" of the work of art as well as in his adolescent reading of Greek tragedy and in his belief in the principle of heredity; the latter belief is alluded to in *ON* and is brought to bear in discussions of the soul in the latter half of "The Critic as Artist." For a discussion of philosophical contradictions in the concept of fate that bear upon Wilde's conception and use of it in the plays, see Benjamin's "Fate and Character," *Illuminations* (304–11).

9. Ellmann, *Wilde*, 13.

10. Quoted in ibid., 33.

11. See Smith and Helfand's "The Context of the Text," one of two illuminating introductory essays to *ON* (6–10). Müller "used [Darwinian] theory to explain the growth of Western languages and . . . accepted Darwin's explanation of the development of nonhuman species," the editors write. "But he differed with Darwin's materialist explanation of human nature and origins. Language, which was inseparable for Müller from all mental activity, was 'the one great barrier between the brute and man.' " The elements of all languages can be traced to phonetic types, Müller argued, which in turn were " 'produced by a power inherent in human nature. They exist, as Plato would say, by nature; though with Plato we should add that, when we say nature, we mean by the hand of God' " (9).

Notes

12. See the editors' commentary on the strength of Ruskin's influence on Wilde (*ON* 14–17).

13. Ellmann, *Wilde*, 50.

14. Unrau suggests that Wilde and Ruskin were better acquainted than is commonly thought.

15. Proust, *On Reading Ruskin*, 38.

16. Harris, *Wilde*, 48.

17. Arthur Symons stresses Pater's social unease and his hatred of every form of extravagance (Symons, introduction to *Renaissance*).

18. Harris, *Wilde*, 104.

19. See preface, n.5. Since Foucault's writing has gained in influence, it has been common to distinguish a modern or late nineteenth-century concept of "homosexuality," entailing a continuous "cultural" identity, from a premodern concept of "sodomy," defined in terms of discrete acts. The word *homosexual* itself did not enter the language until the late nineteenth century. Although a statute declaring sodomy a felony had been in existence since 1533, relations of "gross indecency with another male person" in private—that is, a sexual *relation* as distinguished from a sexual act—were declared a misdemeanor as late as 1885, only ten years before Wilde's conviction. Wilde's generation of actively homosexual men may have been one of the last to conceive of themselves as persons more than as "homosexuals." (See Dowling's *Hellenism and Homosexuality* for a discussion of how the "genuine richness and complexity of late-Victorian psychocultural experience" came to be condensed into a "modern opposition between 'homosexual' and 'heterosexual,'" 134.)

20. Stokes emphasizes Wilde's comparatively bold temperament in an essay on the diaries of George Ives ("Wilde at Bay").

21. In his philosophical parody of Hegel, Kierkegaard writes, "The self is a relation which relates to itself, or that in the relation which is relating to itself. The self is not the relation but the relation's relating to itself" (*Sickness Unto Death* 43).

22. Despite the arresting portrait of Wilde and Gide in Algiers that opens *Sexual Dissidence*, Dollimore's claim that Wilde advocated a "transgressive aesthetic" (derived from consciousness of his homosexuality) is advanced at the expense of *De Profundis*, which, as Dollimore acknowledges, directly contradicts it. To Dollimore, *De Profundis* represents a "tragic defeat of the kind which only ideological coercion, reinforced by overt brutality, can effect. . . . Wilde survives by rescuing an imaginary spiritual autonomy" (95–96). In chapter 4 I argue against this view of *De Profundis* as false consolation. For an answer to the assumption Dollimore makes about artistic genius in general, see Helen Vendler's "Anxiety of Innocence": "Genius is transgressive more by accident—as it strives valiantly towards its intuitions of reality, stumbling along the way over hurdles of convention—than by intent. . . . Transgression, even blasphemy, is incurred as a by-product of accuracy, not as an end in itself" (31). Dollimore's study leaves unanswered larger questions as to whether the "aesthetic" can be *defined* as "transgressive."

23. Vendler, *Music of What Happens*, 286.

24. See Ellmann, *Wilde*, 249–50.

25. West, *Mountain in the Sunlight*, 147.

26. Quoted in Ellmann, *Wilde*, 144–45.

27. Yeats, *Autobiography*, 189.

28. Harris, *Wilde*, 149.

29. Dowling writes: *"Paiderastia, symposia, dialektike* . . . would assume the status of lived categories for Wilde . . . experienced by him on the level of ordinary existence as elements scarcely more remarkable than air or wine" (*Hellenism and Homosexuality* 124).

30. Harris, *Wilde*, 149.

31. Wilde, *Plays*, 331–32.

32. Harris, *Wilde*, 167.

33. Ibid., 150.

34. Ibid., 183.

35. Wilde, *Artist as Critic*, 213.

36. Dowling, *Hellenism and Homosexuality*, 150.

37. Hyde, *Wilde*, 204.

38. Bloom, *Wilde*, 43.

39. Ellmann, *Wilde*, 523.

40. Wilde, *Selected Letters*, 248n.

41. Ellmann, *Wilde*, 430.

42. Yeats, *Autobiography*, 189, 192.

43. Kierkegaard, *Either/Or*, 1:423.

44. "For curiosity's sake he had tried the denial of self" (*DG* 360).

45. Ellmann, *Wilde*, 179.

46. MacIntyre, *Short History of Ethics*, 216.

47. Kierkegaard, *Either/Or*, 2:xviii.

48. Ibid., 2:vii.

49. Ibid., 1:13.

50. Kierkegaard, *Concluding Unscientific Postscript*, 226, 228.

51. Kierkegaard, *Either/Or*, 1:14.

52. Ibid., 1:xii.

53. Wilde, *Selected Letters*, 321. In his essay on Wilde, Joyce invokes "the strange problem of the life of Oscar Wilde" (Critical Writings, 203).

54. Kierkegaard, *Either/Or*, 1:14.

55. In *DP* Wilde writes of the dangers of the aesthetic life, but he also writes (in an 1897 letter) of the dangers to the self when the moral sense is dominant: "I never came across anyone in whom the moral sense was dominant who was not heartless, cruel, vindictive" (*Selected Letters* 321–22).

2. Wilde and His Predecessors

1. See Deleuze, "Nomad Thought."

2. The strength of Wilde's attention to English culture in the formation of his cosmopolitan radicalism is suggested in Small's "Literary Radicalism."

3. See McCormack, *Ascendancy and Tradition*, 228.

4. Worth, *Irish Drama*, 99.

5. Quoted in Texte, *Jean-Jacques Rousseau*, xx.

6. See Wilde's review of Bella Duffy's *Life of Madame de Staël* (*R* 284–86).

Notes

7. This quotation is taken from George Eliot's meditation on history and art in chapter 19 of *Middlemarch* (1872), in which the heroine visits Rome on her wedding journey, a meditation that bears resemblance to Pater's *The Renaissance* (1873). There Pater emphasizes, especially in the beginning, the notion of a Renaissance in the end of the twelfth and the beginning of the thirteenth centuries, a Renaissance "within the middle age itself" (1095). Wilde's cosmopolitanism shows the influence of these readings of history—that is to say, the cosmopolitan is not primarily occupied with separating and distinguishing epochs, and privileging one over the other, as in the case of Ruskin's treatment of the Middle Ages, but in crossing borders of taste and value.

8. See Benjamin's "The Task of the Translator" for commentary on the significance of translation in the Romantic period (*Illuminations* 76).

9. Wordsworth, *Prelude*, 199.

10. Arnold, *Letters*, 189, 156.

11. At the conclusion of chapter 4 of *Culture and Anarchy*, for example, Arnold stresses the need for the English to become more conscious of their Indo-European racial origins. Only by "going back upon the actual instincts and forces which rule our life," can the English find the "clue to some sound order and authority" (*Complete Prose Works*, 5:175).

12. See Hobsbawm's *Age of Empire* for an extended analysis of the relations between nineteenth-century liberalism and war.

13. Wilde's review of Whistler is taken up in the next chapter.

14. In an 1883 lecture to the art students of the Royal Academy, Wilde emphasizes the universal character of art, however much art arises from the nation. "Art is the science of beauty, and Mathematics the science of truth: there is no national school of either. Indeed, a national school is a provincial school, merely" (*M* 311–12). Lecturing in New York in 1882, Wilde claims that art creates "a common intellectual atmosphere between all countries" and that "national hatreds are always strongest where culture is lowest" (*M* 269).

15. Wilde also would have been familiar with the cosmopolitan character of the fifth century Sophists, who wandered from city to city, living on their culture, and establishing *paideia*, the ideal and theory of culture, on a rational basis (see Jaeger, *Paideia*, 1:286–331). The paradoxical emphasis on both individualism and cultural citizenship that characterized their teachings and way of life resembles Wilde's own way of life and philosophy, especially during his lecture-tour in America.

16. Baudelaire, *Selected Writings*, 116.

17. Hennegan, "Personalities and Principles," 189. See also p. 183 for a more detailed discussion of the celebration of Englishness in this period, and Small's *Conditions for Criticism* (138–41).

18. See Baudelaire's critique of eclecticism in "The Salon of 1846" (*Selected Writings* 89–91). "To grasp all is to lose all!" he writes, "to be deep, art demands a constant process of idealization, achieved only at the price of sacrifice." The artist-critic in Wilde who is neither "sincere, reasonable nor fair" owes much to Baudelaire's image of a passionate, keenly focused artist-critic whose "abundant impartiality" serves his "passion" and "appetite." In Wilde and in Baudelaire, "criticism must be partial, passionate . . . must adopt an exclusive point of view, provided always the one adopted opens up the widest horizons" (50). In his review of

Notes

Pater Wilde writes, "for where there is no exaggeration there is no love, and where there is no love there is no understanding. It is only about things that do not interest one, that one can give a really unbiased opinion" (*R* 539).

19. Ellmann, *Wilde*, 204–5.
20. Baudelaire, *Selected Writings*, 116.
21. Ellmann, *Wilde*, 204.
22. Kant, *Perpetual Peace*, 89.
23. Ibid., 34.
24. Ibid., 89.
25. Wilde was also influenced by Arnold and Schiller in his formulation of a cosmopolitan ideal. In "The Function of Criticism at the Present Time," Arnold writes, "The criticism I am really concerned with . . . is a criticism which regards Europe as being, for intellectual and spiritual purposes, one great confederation, bound to a joint action and working to a common result" (*Complete Prose Works*, 3:284). Schiller insisted that the creation of a society which would embody the aesthetic ideal necessitated the transformation of the state. From Schiller and Arnold, both of whom knew Kant's work of course, Wilde derived his emphasis on the social dimension of artistic and intellectual ideals.
26. See *ON* (67, 73), in which the editors draw attention to Wilde's difference from Hegel in his distrust of the inevitability of progressive historical development.
27. Humphrey, translator's introduction to *Perpetual Peace*, 10.
28. Kant, *Critique of Judgment*, 69.
29. Humphrey, translator's introduction to *Perpetual Peace*, 12–13.
30. Kant, *Perpetual Peace*, 41.
31. Baudelaire, *Selected Writings*, 117–18. For important commentary on Baudelaire's influence on Wilde, see Clements's *Baudelaire and the English Tradition*.
32. See n.18, this chapter.
33. See Small, "Literary Radicalism," for a complementary view of Wilde's radicalism.
34. Eagleton, *Ideology of the Aesthetic*, 60–61.
35. Carlyle, "Signs of the Times," 79.
36. Yeats, *Autobiography*, 91.
37. Baudelaire, *My Heart Laid Bare*, 211.
38. Ibid., 177.
39. The editors of *ON* cite Pater's "On Wordsworth" as the immediate source of Wilde's entry (194).
40. Marcus, "Conceptions of the Self," 447.
41. Carlyle, "Signs of the Times," 75.
42. Wilde's deathbed conversion to Catholicism, semi-conscious and with eyes shut, was prompted by Robert Ross, who admited to feelings of guilt for introducing Wilde to homosexuality.
43. In "Literary Radicalism," Small idenitifies the rhetorical methods by which Wilde undermines "the notion of univocal meaning upon which authority, and in particular textual authority, depends" (217).
44. Newman, *Apologia Pro Vita Sua*, 414.
45. Ruskin, *Unto This Last*, 234.

Notes

46. Proust, *On Reading Ruskin*, 51. Proust emphasizes Ruskin's intellectual insincerity, thereby adopting a moral emphasis that has the effect of disguising the real philosophical problems about the relations between the ethical and the aesthetic that lie at the heart of Ruskin's unsatisfactory "compromise." By identifying the problem as one of "sincerity," Proust interprets it ethically, affirming the disparity between ethics and aesthetics that Wilde would gradually work through and overcome.

47. Burne-Jones, quoted in Stanford, ed., *Pre-Raphaelite Writings*, xxvi.

48. Though always willing to praise technical accomplishment in any artist, Wilde's reviews of the Pre-Raphaelites, particularly those of Whistler and Swinburne, contain serious qualifications. Of Swinburne's *Poems and Ballads* (3d series) he writes, "Certainly 'for song's sake' we should love Mr. Swinburne's work, cannot, indeed, help loving it, so marvelous a music-maker is he. But what of the soul? For the soul we must go elsewhere" (*R* 523). Wilde's critique of Whistler's extreme aestheticism is discussed in the next chapter.

49. This is not to deny the obvious influence that the Pre-Raphaelites, and William Morris in particular, had on Wilde's early career, including his lectures in America.

50. In an early review Wilde makes the suggestive recommendation that "Baudelaire might be most advantageously substituted for Keble" (*R* 44), the influential clergyman and poet whose sermon on national apostasy (1833) initiated the Oxford Movement. In "The English Renaissance of Art" Wilde writes, "There is more health in Baudelaire than there is in [Kingsley]" (*M* 262).

51. Wilde, *Artist as Critic*, 190.

52. Ibid., 239.

53. Certain observations in Small's "Literary Radicalism" might be used to cast a new light on "Pen, Pencil, and Poison." Small writes, "The allegation that the authority of an argument was seen to reside in the prestige of the utterer rather than the utterance [a common allegation among Victorian reviewers] has of course a profound irony; the very means by which contemporary critics used to marginalise their arguments proved its validity" (218). Wilde turns this allegation on its head in "Pen, Pencil, and Poison."

54. In an early review in which Wilde lists "books not to be read at all," he includes "all John Stuart Mill, except the essay on *Liberty*" (*R* 43).

55. In something of the same spirit, Nietzsche writes of Mill's "insulting clarity" (*TI* 513).

56. Mill, *Selection of His Works*, 286.

57. Ibid., 279.

58. In this seemingly paradoxical assertion of an individualism that is both "actual" and "potential," an analogy might be made, for example, to a fetus. In *De Profundis* Wilde writes of the individual as a potential "fulfillment of a prophecy." Morris's utopian influence may be seen in these ideas.

59. "The systems that fail are those that rely on the permanency of human nature, and not on its growth and development" (*I* 326).

60. Baudelaire's influence, despite his ill-defined and reactionary leanings, may be felt here. In *My Heart Laid Bare*, he writes, "humanity will progress just as soon as individuals study how to do so" (204). T. S. Eliot's observation on

Baudelaire applies to Wilde as well: "what he knew he found out for himself" ("Introduction" 22). In *De Profundis*, Wilde writes, "Everything must come to one out of one's own nature" (177). "I have to get it all out of myself" (196).

61. Ernst Bendz writes that both of Wilde's friends, Robert Ross and Robert Sherard, assured him that "there is more of Arnold in [Wilde] than of anyone else" (5). See Bendz's discussion of the influence of Arnold's prose style on Wilde (105).

62. Arnold, *Culture and Anarchy, Complete Prose Works*, vol. 5, 224.

63. Ibid., 526.

64. Pater, *Renaissance*, 1129.

65. The differences between Pater and Wilde will be taken up again in later chapters. Pater was still caught in the dualism referred to here in that, as Iser points out, the "relative spirit" that Pater defended and argued for can only be understood as directed against "the system-building efforts permeating the European past" (17). In Pater, art is not a translation of existence (as in Ruskin) but a "treatment" of it, but "treatment" in Pater can only be propagated against "translation." The "aesthetic moment" in Pater gains ascendancy only in opposition to and in the context of ethically-centered systems of the past.

66. Wilde, *Artist as Critic*, 7 (emphasis added).

67. Benjamin, *Reflections*, 271.

3. Wilde's Reassociation of Sensibility

1. I am indebted to the editors of the *Oxford Notebooks* for this phrase (48).

2. James Joyce writes of Wilde's "restless thought that proceeds by sophisms rather than syllogisms" (205)—that is, we may say, by artifice (*sophisma*) rather than by argument.

3. Iser, *Walter Pater*, viii.

4. Smith and Helfand point to Pater's contradictory use of the word *spirit*: "He employs the Hegelian vocabulary of art history but means by 'spirit' only the common characteristics embodied by the art of a period or the collective psychological and emotional needs satisfied by art" (*ON* 231).

5. As shown in the discussion of Wilde's plays in chapter 4, Wilde put this principle into practice. The conventional or "vulgar standard of goodness" of the age was formalized in the Victorian melodrama that Wilde succeeded in transforming.

6. In *The Picture of Dorian Gray*, characters who are victimized by Dorian suffer from his (presumably sexual) vices, but Dorian himself is driven by art, not nature.

7. Arnold, *Culture and Anarchy, Complete Prose Works*, 5:113.

8. On lecture-tour in America (1882), Wilde repeatedly emphasized the importance of decorative art in education. The teaching of decorative arts to children should be included in every curriculum, he argued: "It is a practical school of morals" (*M* 290).

9. See *ON* (71–72) in which the editors of the *Oxford Notebooks* discuss this idea in its relation to Hegel and Pater. See also Spiegelman's *Majestic Indolence*,

chapter 1, for a wide-ranging discussion of some of the sources of Wilde's conception of aesthetic contemplation and criticism.

10. Deleuze writes, "An aphorism is an amalgam of forces that are always held apart from one another" ("Nomad Thought" 145).

11. Although Wilde was acquainted with writers on the continent, such as Gide, who had read French translations of Nietzsche, I can find no references to Nietzsche in Wilde's published writings.

12. Young, *Nietzsche's Philosophy*, 102.

13. Heller, *Importance of Nietzsche*, 127.

14. Unlike Pater, both Gautier and Wilde are acutely conscious of the specific sociological reality against which modern art must struggle, though each conceives of art as intrinsically independent of that reality.

15. In the discussion of Christ as an artist in *De Profundis*, Wilde would affirm a Christian aesthetic but on a new and different basis from that on which he critiques historical Christendom in "The Soul of Man under Socialism" (see chapter 4).

16. Mann, *Last Essays*, 172 and 176. "Nietzsche's Philosophy in Light of Recent History" first appeared in English in 1959. The more recent criticism of Steven Marcus and Philip Rieff offers extensions of Mann's position. Their commentary on Wilde suggests that the unavoidable position to be taken by anyone writing within the tradition of post-war humanist criticism must be moral *as opposed to* aesthetic. Adopting the humanistic point-of-view means accepting the opposition itself. Such oppositions are affirmed because, in Rieff's view, they form the very basis of culture, despite and because of the fact they are repressive. (No one understood this better than Wilde.)

4. Wilde's Philosophy of Art

1. In *The Picture of Dorian Gray*, a character comments, "Well, the way of paradoxes is the way of truth. To test Reality we must see it on a tight-rope. When the Verities become acrobats we can judge them" (63).

2. See Stokes's *In the Nineties* (161–66) for important historical background on Wilde's attitude towards journalists and journalism.

3. Benjamin, *Reflections*, 89.

4. Ibid.

5. Nietzsche articulates this contradiction in a passage in *Twilight of the Idols* (529). There he comes close to Wilde in his resolution of the question when he emphasizes art's power to stimulate life.

6. Again the contrast with Nietzsche's condemnation of the critical spirit (as "Alexanderianism," etc.) is instructive.

7. Benjamin, *Illuminations*, 83–84.

8. Ibid., 156.

9. Arnold, "Study of Poetry," *Complete Prose Works*, 9:161–62.

10. Ibid., 548.

11. Lecturing in America in 1882, Wilde said, "By keeping aloof from the social problems of the day . . . [art] more completely realises for us that which we desire. For to most of us the real life is the life we do not lead" (*M* 256).

Notes

12. Benjamin, *Reflections*, 183–84.

13. Pater, *Renaissance*, 1094.

14. See Benjamin's "A Small History of Photography" (*One-Way Street* 250). Benjamin read *The Picture of Dorian Gray* as a student in 1912 and wrote in a letter to Herbert Belmore, "It is perfect and a dangerous book" (*Correspondence* 16).

15. Gide, *Wilde*, 4–5. It is typical of Wilde in this early period to make a radical distinction between "art" and "life" ("there are two worlds"), at the same time that he hints of their connection through an idea of reception ("the one which has to be talked about [the world of art] because it would not exist otherwise.") In his words to Gide, Wilde is suggesting both that daily life cannot be redeemed and that it can—by being brought to life through the consciousness of art.

16. Vendler, *Music of What Happens*, 4.

17. See T. S. Eliot's "Arnold and Pater," 390.

18. "The drama is the meeting-place of art and life," said Wilde in 1882 (*M* 264).

19. See the work of Powell, Raby, Stokes (*Resistable Theatres*), and Worth.

20. See Mikhail's "The French Influence on Oscar Wilde's Comedies," which explores the influences of Sardou and Dumas *fils* on Wilde's plays.

21. Wilde, *Lady Windermere's Fan*, 167. (Page numbers are for *The First Collected Edition of the Works of Oscar Wilde*.)

22. Benjamin, *Reflections*, 306–7.

23. Wilde, *Lady Windermere's Fan*, 165.

24. Wilde, *An Ideal Husband*, 228.

25. Wilde, *The Importance of Being Earnest*, 109.

26. Ibid., 35.

27. Benjamin, *Reflections*, 314.

28. Wilde, *The Importance of Being Earnest*, 76–77.

29. Wilde, *Selected Letters*, 348.

30. Adorno, *Notes to Literature*, 2:248.

31. Epifanio San Juan's comment on the play.

32. Ellmann, *Wilde*, 429.

33. Ibid.

34. Said, *The World*, 43.

35. Hyde, *Three Trials*, 123.

36. Fraser, *Beauty and Belief*, 226.

37. The following anecdote suggests Wilde's attitude toward formal conversion: once, when Robert Ross insisted that Wilde convert in his last years, Wilde asked to see a priest. But Ross, sensing that Wilde was not serious, did not follow through. Clearly Wilde, though he cared for Ross deeply, was amused by the incident, thereafter dubbing him: " 'the cherub with the flaming sword, forbidding my entrance into Eden.' " Later, after the barely conscious Wilde converted on his deathbed at Ross's prompting, Ross confessed, "I did it for my own conscience" (Ellmann, *Wilde*, 583, 584).

38. Joyce, *Critical Writings*, 203–5. Harold Bloom, one of the few critics of Wilde to recognize the seriousness of Wilde's conception of Christ as an artist, writes that this conception was "not in Wilde a frivolous belief but an heretical one, indeed an aesthetic version of Gnosticism" (3). My own understanding of this conception is indebted to conversations with Howard Eiland.

39. Quoted in Ellmann, *Wilde*, 583.
40. Wilde, *Selected Letters*, 352.
41. Hegel's influence is felt in these ideas. See "The Redemptive History of Christ" in Hegel's *Aesthetics* (1:534–35), in which Hegel discusses Christ as the self-conscious representative of romantic art.
42. Kant, *Perpetual Peace*, 29.
43. Baudelaire, *Selected Writings*, 116.
44. Ibid.
45. Kierkegaard, *Either/Or*, 2:xvi.
46. In the passage quoted from *De Profundis*, Wilde approaches the concept of despair in Kierkegaard's *The Sickness Unto Death*: "Not being in despair may exactly be to be in despair" (55); the "horror" of despair lies in "its hiddenness" (57).
47. Parallels to this idea are found in Pater's *Greek Studies* and Nietzsche's *The Birth of Tragedy*.
48. Harris, *Wilde*, 579.
49. Pfefferkorn, *Novalis*, 222.
50. Wilde, *Selected Letters*, 277.
51. Ellmann, *Wilde*, 578.

Epilogue

1. Gide, *Wilde*, 2.
2. Yeats, *Autobiography*, 87.
3. Benjamin, *Illuminations*, 83.
4. Lecturing in America in 1882, Wilde repeatedly emphasized that "bad art is a great deal worse than no art at all" (*M* 285). See also "The Critic as Artist" (*I* 130–31).
5. In "The Soul of Man under Socialism," in which Wilde propounds his theory of reception most concretely, he compares the reader to a violin on which the artist plays (*I* 317). For related commentary on the possibilities of aesthetic receptivity, see Spiegelman's discussion of Kant (*Majestic Indolence* 18–19).
6. Lines from a draft epilogue of the 1861 edition of *Fleurs du Mal*, published posthumously in 1869. The translation is by Arthur Symons.
7. In his essay on Karl Kraus, Benjamin writes of "that solidarity of the man of letters with the whore to which Baudelaire's existence is once again the most inviolable testimony" (*Reflections* 258).
8. See Wilde, *Selected Letters*, 96, for an interesting, early explanation of this aphorism. See also Baudelaire's "Of Virtuous Plays and Novels": "Is art useful? Yes. Why? Because it is art" (*Selected Writings* 110–11).
9. Adorno, *Notes to Literature*, 2:248.
10. Mill, *On Liberty*, 130.

❧ Select Bibliography

Adorno, Theodor W. *Minima Moralia: Reflections from a Damaged Life.* Trans. E. F. N. Jephcott. London: New Left Books, 1974.

———. *Notes to Literature.* 2 vols. Trans. Shierry Weber Nicholsen. New York: Columbia Univ. Press, 1974.

Arnold, Matthew. *The Complete Prose Works of Matthew Arnold.* Ed. R. H. Super. 11 vols. Ann Arbor: Univ. of Michigan Press, 1960–77.

———. *The Letters of Matthew Arnold.* Vol. 1, *1829–1859.* Ed. Cecil Y. Lang. Charlottesville: Univ. Press of Virginia, 1996.

Auden, W. H. "Playboy of the Western World: St. Oscar the Homintern Martyr." In *The New Partisan Reader, 1945–1953,* ed. William Phillips and Philip Rahv. New York: Harcourt, Brace, 1953.

Bashford, Bruce. "Arnold and Wilde: Criticism as Humanistic." *English Literature in Transition* 3 (1985): 137–49.

Baudelaire, Charles. *My Heart Laid Bare.* Ed. Peter Quennel. Trans. Norman Cameron. New York: Haskell House, 1975.

———. *The Prose Poems and La Fanfarlo.* Trans. Rosemary Lloyd. New York: Oxford Univ. Press, 1991.

———. *Selected Writings on Art and Literature.* Trans. P. E. Charvet. London: Penguin, 1972.

Beckson, Karl, ed. *Aesthetes and Decadents of the 1890s.* New York: Random House, 1966.

———, ed. *Oscar Wilde: The Critical Heritage.* London: Routledge and Kegan Paul, 1970.

Bell-Villada, Gene H. *Art for Art's Sake and Literary Life: How Politics and Markets Helped Shape the Ideology and Culture of Aestheticism, 1790–1990.* Lincoln: Univ. of Nebraska Press, 1996.

Bendz, Ernst. *The Influence of Pater and Matthew Arnold in the Prose Writings of Oscar Wilde.* London: H. Grevel, 1914.

Benjamin, Walter. *The Correspondence of Walter Benjamin, 1910–1940.* Ed. Gershom Scholem and Theodor W. Adorno. Trans. Manfred R. Jacobson and Evelyn M. Jacobson. Chicago: Univ. of Chicago Press, 1994.

Select Bibliography

————. *Illuminations*. Trans. Harry Zohn. New York: Schocken Books, 1968.

————. *One-Way Street and Other Writings*. Trans. Edmund Jephcott and Kingsley Shorter. London: Verso, 1979.

————. *Reflections*. Trans. Edmund Jephcott. New York: Schocken Books, 1986.

Bloom, Harold, ed. *Oscar Wilde: Modern Critical Views*. New York: Chelsea House, 1985.

Bromwich, David. *A Choice of Inheritance: Self and Community from Edmund Burke to Robert Frost*. Cambridge: Harvard Univ. Press, 1989.

Buckler, William E. "Building a Bulwark against Despair: 'The Critic as Artist.' " *English Literature in Transition* 32 (1989): 279–89.

Buckley, Jerome. *The Turning Key: Autobiography and the Subjective Impulse since 1800*. Cambridge: Harvard Univ. Press, 1984.

Campos, Christophe. *The View of France from Arnold to Bloomsbury*. London: Oxford Univ. Press, 1965.

Camus, Albert. *Oscar Wilde: "Ballade de la geole de Reading."* Paris: Falaize, 1952.

Carlyle, Thomas. *The Life of Friedrich Schiller*. London: Chapman and Hall, 1869.

————. "Signs of the Times." In *Selected Writings*, ed. Alan Shelston. London: Penguin Books, 1971.

Chamberlin, J. E. *Ripe Was the Drowsy Hour*. New York: Seabury, 1977.

Clements, Patricia. *Baudelaire and the English Tradition*. Princeton: Princeton Univ. Press, 1985.

Cohen, Philip K. *The Moral Vision of Oscar Wilde*. London: Associated Univ. Press, 1978.

Crossley, Ceri, and Ian Small, eds. *Studies in Anglo-French Cultural Relations*. London: Macmillan, 1988.

Deleuze, Giles. "Nomad Thought." In *The New Nietzsche*, ed. David B. Allison. New York: Delta, 1977.

Dellamora, Richard. *Masculine Desire: The Sexual Politics of Victorian Aestheticism*. Chapel Hill: Univ. of North Carolina Press, 1990.

Dollimore, Jonathan. *Sexual Dissidence: Augustine to Wilde, Freud to Foucault*. Oxford: Clarendon Press, 1991.

Dowling, Linda. *Hellenism and Homosexuality in Victorian Oxford*. Ithaca: Cornell Univ. Press, 1994.

————. *Language and Decadence in the Victorian Fin de Siècle*. Princeton: Princeton Univ. Press, 1986.

Eagleton, Terry. *The Ideology of the Aesthetic*. Oxford: Basil Blackwell, 1990.

Eliot, George. *Middlemarch*. London: Penguin, 1965.

Eliot, T. S. "Arnold and Pater." In *Selected Essays*. New York: Harcourt, Brace, and World, 1932.

————. Introduction to *Intimate Journals*, by Charles Baudelaire. Trans. Christopher Isherwood. Westport CT: Hyperion Press, 1978.

Ellmann, Richard. Introduction to *The Artist as Critic: Critical Writings of Oscar Wilde*. Chicago: Univ. of Chicago Press, 1968.

————. *Oscar Wilde*. New York: Alfred A. Knopf, 1988.

Engels, Friedrich. "On the History of Early Christianity." In *Basic Writings on Politics and Philosophy*, ed. Lewis S. Feuer. New York: Doubleday, 1959.

Select Bibliography

Fleishman, Avrom. *Figures of Autobiography: The Language of Self-Writing in Victorian and Modern England.* Berkeley: Univ. of California Press, 1983.

Fletcher, Ian, and John Stokes. *The Decadent Consciousness.* New York: Garland, 1979.

———, and John Stokes. "Oscar Wilde." In *Anglo-Irish Literature: A Review of Research,* ed. Richard J. Finneran. New York: MLA, 1976.

———, and John Stokes. "Oscar Wilde." In *Recent Research on Anglo-Irish Writers: A Supplement to Anglo-Irish Literature: A Review of Research,* ed. Richard J. Finneran. New York: MLA, 1983.

Forster, E. M. *Howards End.* New York: Random House, 1921.

Foucault, Michel. *The History of Sexuality.* Vol. 1, *An Introduction.* Trans. Robert Hurley. New York: Vintage Books, 1988.

Fraser, Hilary. *Beauty and Belief: Aesthetics and Religion in Victorian Literature.* Cambridge: Cambridge Univ. Press, 1986.

Freedman, Jonathan. *Professions of Taste: Henry James, British Aestheticism and Commodity Culture.* Stanford: Stanford Univ. Press, 1990.

Gagnier, Regenia A. *Idylls of the Marketplace: Oscar Wilde and the Victorian Public.* Aldershot: Scolar Press, 1987.

Gide, André. *Oscar Wilde.* Trans. Bernard Frechtman. New York: Philosophical Library, 1949.

Gordon, Jan B. " 'Decadent Spaces': Notes for a Phenomenology of the Fin de Siècle." In *Decadence and the 1890s,* ed. Ian Fletcher and Malcolm Bradbury. London: Edward Arnold, 1979.

Guy, Josephine M. *The British Avant-Garde: The Theory and Politics of Tradition.* London: Harvester-Wheatsheaf, 1991.

Harris, Frank. *Oscar Wilde: His Life and Confessions.* 2 vols. New York, 1918.

Hegel, G. W. F. *Aesthetics: Lectures on Fine Arts.* 2 vols. Trans. T. M. Knox. Oxford: Oxford Univ. Press, 1975.

Heller, Erich. *The Importance of Nietzsche.* Chicago: Univ. of Chicago Press, 1988.

Hennegan, Alison. "Personalities and Principles: Aspects of Literature and Life in Fin-de-Siècle England." In *Fin de Siècle and its Legacy,* ed. Mikulas Teich and Roy Porter. Cambridge: Cambridge Univ. Press, 1990.

Hobsbawm, Eric. *Age of Empire, 1875–1914.* New York: Pantheon, 1987.

Humphrey, Ted. Translator's introduction to *Perpetual Peace and Other Essays,* by Immanuel Kant. Indianapolis: Hackett Publishing, 1983.

Hyde, H. Montgomery. *Oscar Wilde: A Biography.* New York: Farrar, Strauss and Giroux, 1975.

———, ed. *The Three Trials of Oscar Wilde.* New York: Univ. Books, 1948.

Iser, Wolfgang. *Walter Pater: The Aesthetic Moment.* Trans. David Wilson. Cambridge: Cambridge Univ. Press, 1987.

Jackson, Russell, ed. *Oscar Wilde, The Importance of Being Earnest.* London: Benn, 1980.

Jaeger, Werner. *Paideia: The Ideals of Greek Culture.* Vol. 1. Trans. Gilbert Highet. New York: Oxford Univ. Press, 1939.

Jenkyns, Richard. *The Victorians and Ancient Greece.* Oxford: Blackwell, 1980.

Joyce, James. *The Critical Writings of James Joyce.* Ed. Ellsworth Mason and Richard Ellmann. New York: Viking, 1959.

Select Bibliography

Kant, Immanuel. *Critique of Judgment.* Trans. J. H. Bernard. New York: Hafner Press, 1951.

———. *Critique of Pure Reason.* Trans. Norman Kemp Smith. New York: St Martin's Press, 1965.

———. *Perpetual Peace and Other Essays.* Trans. Ted Humphrey. Indianapolis: Hackett, 1983.

Karl, Frederick R. *Modern and Modernism: The Sovereignty of the Artist: 1885–1925.* New York: Macmillan, 1985.

Kermode, Frank. *Romantic Image.* London: Routledge and Kegan Paul, 1957.

Kierkegaard, Søren. *Concluding Unscientific Postscript.* Trans. David F. Swenson and Walter Lowrie. Princeton: Princeton Univ. Press, 1941.

———. *Either/Or.* 2 vols. Trans. David F. Swenson and Lillian Marvin Swenson. New York: Anchor Books, 1959.

———. *The Sickness Unto Death.* Trans. Alistair Hannay. New York: Penguin, 1989.

Knox, Melissa. *Oscar Wilde: A Long and Lovely Suicide.* New Haven: Yale Univ. Press, 1994.

Kohl, Norbert. *Oscar Wilde: The Works of a Conformist Rebel.* Trans. David Henry Wilson. Cambridge: Cambridge Univ. Press, 1989.

MacIntyre, Alasdair. *A Short History of Ethics.* New York: Macmillan, 1966.

Mann, Thomas. *Last Essays.* Trans. Richard and Clara Winston and Tania and James Stern. New York: Alfred A. Knopf, 1966.

Marcus, Steven. "Conceptions of the Self in an Age of Progress." In *Progress and Its Discontents,* ed. Gabriel A. Almond, Marvin Chodorow, and Roy Harvey Pearce. Berkeley: Univ. of California Press, 1982.

McCormack, W. J. *Ascendancy and Tradition in Anglo-Irish Literary History.* Oxford: Clarendon Press, 1985.

Meisel, Perry. *The Myth of the Modern: A Study in British Literature and Criticism after 1850.* New Haven: Yale Univ. Press, 1987.

Mikhail, E. H. "The French Influence on Oscar Wilde's Comedies." *Revue de litterature comparee* 42 (1968): 220–33.

———, ed. *Oscar Wilde: Interviews and Recollections.* 2 vols. London: Macmillan, 1979.

Mill, John Stuart. *On Liberty.* London: Penguin, 1985.

———. *A Selection of His Works.* Ed. John M. Robson. New York: Macmillan, 1985.

Monneyron, Frederic. "Une lecture Nietscheene de Dorian Gray." *Cahiers Victoriennes et Edwardiennes* 16 (1982): 139–45.

Murray, Isobel, ed. *Oscar Wilde.* Oxford: Oxford Univ. Press, 1989.

Nassaar, Christopher S. *Into the Demon Universe: A Literary Exploration of Oscar Wilde.* New Haven: Yale Univ. Press, 1974.

Newman, John Henry. *Apologia Pro Vita Sua.* In *Victorian Literature: Prose,* ed. G. B. Tennyson and Donald J. Gray. New York: Macmillan, 1976.

Nietzsche, Friedrich. *The Antichrist.* In *The Portable Nietzsche,* trans. Walter Kaufman. New York: Viking, 1954.

———. *Beyond Good and Evil.* Trans. Marianne Cowan. Chicago: Gateway Edition, 1955.

———. *Joyful Wisdom.* Trans. Thomas Common. New York: Frederick Ungar, 1960.

Select Bibliography

———. *On the Genealogy of Morals and Ecce Homo*. Trans. Walter Kaufman. New York: Random House, 1969.

———. *Thus Spoke Zarathustra*. Trans. R. J. Hollingdale. Baltimore: Penguin, 1961.

———. *Twilight of the Idols*. In *The Portable Nietzsche*, ed. Walter Kaufmann. New York: Viking, 1954.

———. *The Will to Power*. Trans. Walter Kaufmann and R. J. Hollingdale. New York: Random House, 1968.

Nussbaum, Martha. "Patriotism or Cosmopolitanism?" *Boston Review* 19 (Oct./ Nov. 1994): 3–6.

Pater, Walter. *The Renaissance*. In *Victorian Literature: Prose*, ed. G. B. Tennyson and Donald J. Gray. New York: Macmillan, 1976.

Paul, Charles B., and Robert D. Pepper. "The Importance of Reading Alfred: Oscar Wilde's Debt to Alfred de Musset." *Bulletin of the New York Public Library* 75 (1971): 506–42.

Pfefferkorn, Kristin. *Novalis: A Romantic's Theory of Language and Poetry*. New Haven: Yale Univ. Press, 1988.

Powell, Kerry. *Oscar Wilde and the Theatre of the 1890s*. Cambridge: Cambridge Univ. Press, 1990.

Proust, Marcel. *On Reading Ruskin*. Trans. Jean Autret, William Burford, and Phillip J. Wolfe. New Haven: Yale Univ. Press, 1987.

Raafat, Z. "The Literary Indebtedness of Wilde's *Salomé* to Sardou's *Theodora*." *Revue de litterature comparee* 40 (1966): 453–66.

Raby, Peter. *Oscar Wilde*. Cambridge: Cambridge Univ. Press, 1988.

"Replies to Nussbaum." *Boston Review* 20 (Feb./March 1995): 10–17.

Rieff, Philip. "The Impossible Culture: Wilde as a Modern Prophet." *Salmagundi* 58 (1983): 406–26.

Riquelme, John Paul. "Shalom/Solomon/Salomé: Modernism and Wilde's Aesthetic Politics." *Centennial Review* 13 (1995): 575–610.

Roditi, Edouard. *Oscar Wilde*. Norfolk CT: New Directions, 1947.

Ruskin, John. *Unto This Last and Other Writing*. Ed. Clive Wilmer. London: Penguin Books, 1985.

Said, Edward. *The World, the Text, and the Critic*. Cambridge: Harvard Univ. Press, 1983.

San Juan, Epifanio. *The Art of Oscar Wilde*. Princeton: Princeton Univ. Press, 1967.

Schiller, Friedrich. *On the Aesthetic Education of Man*. Ed. and Trans. Elizabeth M. Wilkinson and L. A. Willoughby. Oxford: Clarendon Press, 1967.

Schmidgall, Gary. *The Stranger Wilde*. New York: Dutton, 1994.

Schwarz, Stanley. "The Influence of Dumas Fils on Oscar Wilde." *French Review* 7 (1933): 5–25.

Shaw, G. B. *Dramatic Opinions and Essays*. London: Constable, 1907.

Shelley, Andrew. "Defining Wilde." *Essays in Criticism* 38, no. 2 (1988): 156–61.

Shewan, Rodney. *Oscar Wilde: Art and Egotism*. London: Macmillan, 1977.

Small, Ian, ed. *The Aesthetes*. London: Routledge and Kegan Paul, 1979.

———. *Conditions for Criticism: Authority, Knowledge, and Literature in the Late Nineteenth Century*. Oxford: Clarendon Press, 1991.

———. "Literary Radicalism in the British Fin de Siècle." In *Fin de Siècle/Fin du Globe*, ed. John Stokes. New York: St. Martin's Press, 1992.

Select Bibliography

————. *Oscar Wilde Revalued*. Greensboro NC: ELT Press, 1993.

Spiegelman, Willard. *Majestic Indolence: English Romantic Poetry and the Work of Art*. New York and Oxford: Oxford Univ. Press, 1995.

Stanford D., ed. *Pre-Raphaelite Writings*. London: J. M. Dent, 1973.

Stokes, John. *In the Nineties*. London: Harvester-Wheatsheaf, 1990.

————. *Resistable Theatres*. London: Paul Elek, 1972.

————. "Wilde at Bay: the Diaries of George Ives." *English Literature in Transition* 26 (1983): 175–86.

Symons, Arthur. Introduction to *The Renaissance*, by Walter Pater. New York: Modern Library, 1954.

Texte, Joseph. *Jean-Jacques Rousseau and the Cosmopolitan Spirit in Literature*. Trans. J. W. Matthews. New York: Burt Franklin, 1970.

Trilling, Lionel. *Sincerity and Authenticity*. Cambridge: Harvard Univ. Press, 1971.

Turner, Frank. *The Greek Heritage in Victorian Britain*. New Haven: Yale Univ. Press, 1981.

Unrau, John. "Ruskin and the Wildes: the Whitelands Connection." *Notes and Queries* 29 (1982): 316–17.

Vendler, Helen. "Anxiety of Innocence." *The New Republic* 209 (Nov. 1993): 27–34.

————. *The Music of What Happens*. Cambridge: Harvard Univ. Press, 1988.

Watson, Edward A. "Wilde's Iconoclastic Classicism: 'The Critic as Artist.'" *English Literature in Transition* 27 (1984): 225–35.

Weeks, Jeffrey. *Coming Out: Homosexual Politics in Britain from the Nineteenth Century to the Present*. London: Quartet, 1977.

Weil, Simone. *Gravity and Grace*. Trans. Gustave Thibon. New York: Octagon Books, 1983.

West, Alick. *The Mountain in the Sunlight: Studies in Conflict and Unity*. London: Lawrence and Wishart, 1958.

Wilde, Oscar. *The Artist as Critic: Critical Writings of Oscar Wilde*. Ed. Richard Ellmann. Chicago: Univ. of Chicago Press, 1968.

————. *The First Collected Edition of the Works of Oscar Wilde*. Ed. Robert Ross. 15 vols. London: Methuen and Co., 1908; rpt. Dawsons of Pall Mall, 1969.

————. *Oscar Wilde's Oxford Notebooks: A Portrait of a Mind in the Making*. Ed. Philip E. Smith and Michael S. Helfand. New York: Oxford Univ. Press, 1989.

————. *Plays*. New York: Penguin, 1977.

————. *Selected Letters of Oscar Wilde*. Ed. Rupert Hart-Davis. Oxford: Oxford Univ. Press, 1979.

Willoughby, Guy. *Art and Christhood: The Aesthetics of Oscar Wilde*. London: Associated Univ. Presses, 1993.

Wimsatt, William K., and Cleanth Brooks. *Literary Criticism: A Short History*. New York: Random House, 1957.

Wordsworth, William. *The Prelude or the Growth of a Poet's Mind* (1805 text). Ed. Ernest Selincourt. London: Oxford Univ. Press, 1964.

Worth, Katherine. *The Irish Drama of Europe from Yeats to Beckett*. London: Athlone Press, 1978.

Yeats, William Butler. *The Autobiography of William Butler Yeats*. New York: Macmillan, 1965.

Young, Julian. *Nietzsche's Philosophy of Art*. Cambridge: Cambridge Univ. Press, 1992.

✸ Index

Index

Index

Engels, Friedrich, 31, 58
"Epilogue" (Baudelaire), 110
Ethics, The (Aristotle), 17
evolution, Wilde's idealist interpretation of, 6
experience, 73, 77

fairy tales, Wilde's, 107
"Fate and Character" (Benjamin), 85
fate, 6, 17, 54, 85–87
Feeling for Nature in Scottish Poetry, The,
    Wilde's review of, 25
Fichte, Johann Gottlieb, 28
fiction, 37, 71–72, 77; Russian, 43; versus lying, 60, 69; Victorian, 88–89
fire as metaphor, 48, 49
Flaubert, Gustave, *Herodias,* 83
"Fleshly School of Poetry, The" (Buchanan), 44
Fletcher, Ian, *Oscar Wilde,* 113 n.4
Fleurs du Mal, Les (Baudelaire), 43
form, 1, 53, 54
Forster, E. M., 27
Foucault, Michel, 116 n.19
France, 29, 36, 48, 65
Fraser, Hilary, 96
Frederick, 28
Freedman, Jonathan, *Professions of Taste,*
    113–14 n.6
French Revolution, the, 26, 76
Freud, Sigmund, 48
"Function of Criticism at the Present Time, The" (Arnold), 119 n.25

Gagnier, Regenia A., *Idylls of the Marketplace,* 113 n.6
Gautier, Théophile, 60
German thought, 28, 105
Germany, Wilde's reputation in, 113 n.4
Gide, André, 14, 17, 23, 39, 58, 78, 91
Gilbert and Sullivan, *Patience,* 107
God, 40, 41
Goethe, Johann Wolfgang von, 28–29, 65
Gosse, Edmund, 29
Gothic, 30; Ruskin's preference for, 9, 42
Gravity and Grace (Weil), 91
Great Expectations (Dickens), 88

Greece, 7, 59
Greeks, ancient, 6, 28, 41, 58, 61
Greek Studies (Pater), 124 n.47
Greenaway, Kate, 42

Harris, Frank, 9, 10, 12, 14, 17, 63, 105
Hebraism, xvi, 36, 48
Hegel, Georg, 33, 50
Helfand, Michael S., xv, 33, 115 n.11
Hellenism, xvi, 36, 48, 58
Hellenism (Dowling), 113 n.5
Heller, Erich, 59
Herodias (Flaubert), 83
Hinksey Road experiment, 42
homosexuality: and bunburying, 90;
    Pater's, 9; Ross's, 10; Wilde's, xiv, 1,
    10, 11, 17
Howards End (Forster), 27
Hume, David, xvii, 53
humor, 85–86, 89
Humphrey, Ted, 34
Huysmans, Joris-Karl, 67

Ibsen, Heinrich, 84
"Idea for a Universal History with a Cosmopolitan Intent" (Kant), 32
Ideal Husband, An (Wilde), 83, 86
idealism, 6, 7; Kant's, xvii, 33; Ruskin's,
    8, 42; Wilde's, 47, 62–63
Ideology of the Aesthetic (Eagleton), 37
Idylls of the Marketplace (Gagnier), 113 n.6
imagination, 73–74
Importance of Being Earnest, The
    (Wilde), 11, 12, 23, 83–85, 87–91
inevitability of art, 5
Intentions and the Soul of Man (Wilde),
    xvii, 12, 49, 93
In the Nineties (Stokes), 114 n.7
Iser, Wolfgang, 53
Ives, George, 116 n.20

James, Henry, 19, 56
Johnson, Lionel, 12
Johnson, Samuel, 60
journalism, 71, 75, 111
"Journals and Notebook" (Baudelaire), 38

133

Index

Index

"Of Virtuous Plays and Novels" (Baudelaire), 124 n.8
On Liberty (Mill), 30, 45–46
On the Aesthetic Education of Man (Schiller), 1
On the Genealogy of Morals (Nietzsche), 72
"On the Proverb" (Kant), 32
Oscar, the, 31
Oscar Wilde (Fletcher and Stokes), 113 n.4
Oscar Wilde Revalued (Small), 113 n.4
Oxford, 9, 10; Wilde at, xv, xvii, 6, 7, 10, 28–29, 32–34, 38, 40, 51, 58, 60; and Wilde's interpretation of evolution, 6
Oxford Notebooks (Wilde), xv, 7–8, 38, 53

Paideia (Jaeger), 118 n.15
pain, 42, 46–47, 61, 82, 84, 87, 90, 103
Palace of Art, 32
Paris, Wilde in, 5, 11, 16, 22, 23
Pater, Walter, xiv, 8–10, 15, 18–19, 33, 36, 49, 50, 53, 60–61, 66, 76; Wilde's debt to, xvii, 3, 38; conclusion to *The Renaissance*, xvii, 3, 19, 39, 59; Wilde's review of, 62; *Greek Studies*, 124 n.47
Patience (Gilbert and Sullivan), 107
"Pen, Pencil and Poison" (Wilde), 44
Persuasion (Austen), 37
Picture of Dorian Gray, The (Wilde), xviii, 9, 11, 12, 15, 18, 19, 29, 56, 77–82, 88, 93, 94
Pilgrim's Progress, The (Bunyan), 40
Plato, 12, 13, 15, 48, 50, 55, 56, 64; and evil, xix; *Laws*, 90; and Wilde's definition of art, 3
pleasure, 61, 63, 70, 74, 84, 87, 90
Poems (Wilde), 12
Poems and Ballads (Swinburne), 120 n.48
politics, 30, 32, 36, 81, 86
Portora Royal School, 1, 2
"Portrait of Mr. W. H., The" (Wilde), 9, 12, 14, 15, 56, 76–77
positivism, 28, 66
poverty, 47, 84, 96
Powell, Kerry, 84
Pre-Raphaelites, 41, 42, 43, 61

prison, 2, 4, 6, 11, 16, 21, 40, 58, 62–63, 96, 104
Professions of Taste (Freedman), 113–14 n.6
prose writers, Victorian, 26–27, 36; Wilde's debt to, 3, 65
Protestantism, 40, 48
Proust, Marcel, 8, 41, 42
providence, divine, 101

Queensberry, Marquess of, 17, 92–93

Reading Gaol, xix, 84
reception, 2, 72
receptivity, 60, 82–83
Redgrave, Michael, 89
"Remarkable Rocket, The" (Wilde), 108
Renaissance, English, of art, 76
Renaissance, The (Pater), 3, 53, 76; conclusion to, xvii, 3, 19, 49, 59
Renaissance, the, art of, 43, 61
Renan, Ernest, 97
Rieff, Philip, 122 n.16
Roditi, Edouard, xiv, xix
romanticism, 26, 62, 73
Romantic period, 118 n.8
Ross, Robert, 10, 17
Rossetti, Dante Gabriel, 44
Rousseau, Jean-Jacques, 26, 30
Royal Academy, xix
Ruskin, John, xviii, 3, 8–9, 30, 36, 41, 42, 55, 66, 75, 81, 84

Said, Edward, 92
Saint Francis of Assisi, 96
Salomé (Wilde), 12, 29, 83–84
Sand, George, 41
Sartor Resartus (Carlyle), 11
Sartre, Jean-Paul, *No Exit*, 91
Schiller, Friedrich, xiii, xviii, 1; *On the Aesthetic Education of Man*, 1; *Letters on Aesthetic Education*, 17–18; use of art and life, 2
Schlegel, A. W., 26
Schlegel, Friedrich, 77
Schlegel family (Forster, *Howards End*), 27

Index

Schmidgall, Gary, 113 n.5
Schopenhauer, Arthur, 61
second reform bill, 67
secrecy, 92
sentimentalism, 63, 95
Sex and Character (Weininger), 62
Sexual Dissidence (Dollimore), 114 n.6
Shakespeare, William, 26; plays, 15, 75, 82; sonnets, 76
Shaw, George Bernard, 27, 90
Sherard, Robert, 11
Sickness Unto Death, The (Kierkegaard), 124 n.46
"Signs of the Times" (Carlyle), xvi, 36, 37, 39
Small, Ian, 113 n.4, 114 nn.7–8
Smith, Philip E., xv, 33, 115 n.11
social class, 81
social determinism, 88
sodomy, 116 n.19
Sorrento, Wilde in, 5
soul, 81, 96
"Soul of Man under Socialism, The" (Wilde), 7, 10, 23, 30–31, 36, 39, 42, 44, 47, 61, 63, 82–84, 87
spectatorship, 97
Spencer, Herbert, 28
Spengler, Oswald, 62
Spiegelman, Willard, *Majestic Indolence*, 121–22 n.9
Staël, Madame de, 26, 29, 41
Stanislavsky, Konstantin, 87
state, the, 48
"Stealthy School of Criticism, The" (Rossetti), 44
Stevenson, Robert Louis, *The Strange Case of Dr. Jekyl and Mr. Hyde*, 13–14
Stokes, John, 113 nn. 4–5, 114 n.7
"Storyteller, The" (Benjamin), 71
Strange Case of Dr. Jekyl and Mr. Hyde, The (Stevenson), 13–14
strength as metaphor, 48, 49
Studies in the Greek Poets (Symonds), 7
"Study of Poetry, The" (Arnold), 74
sun, the, 91
"Sun Rising, The" (Donne), 92

sweetness as metaphor, 44, 48, 49, 58
Swinburne, Algernon Charles, 7, 44; 120 n.48
symbol, 80, 101
symbolists, 75, 83
Symonds, J. A., *Studies in the Greek Poets*, 7
Symons, Arthur, 29
syphilis, 115 n.8

Task of the Translator, The (Benjamin), 118 n.8
Thackeray, William, 60
Thus Spoke Zarathustra (Nietzsche), 102
Tolstoi, Leo, 56
Traffic (Ruskin), 41
tragedy, 52, 82–83, 115 n.8
trials, xviii, 2, 14–17, 19, 62, 70, 91, 94
Trilling, Lionel, xiv
Trinity College, Dublin, Wilde at, xvii, 6
Trotsky, Leon, 26
truth, xviii, 4, 48, 50, 58–59, 80, 92–94; metaphysical, 75; problem of, 70–71; and things as they are, 2
"Truth of Masks, The" (Wilde), 75
Turner, Reginald, 90
Turning Key, The (Buckley), 115 n.2
Twilight of the Idols (Nietzsche), 122 n.5

Unto This Last (Ruskin), 42
utilitarianism, 28, 46–47, 54, 58, 63, 82

Vendler, Helen, 11, 80; "Anxiety of Innocence," 116 n.22
Verlaine, Paul, 29
Victorians, the, 36, 63; ethics, 24, 64; faith in human development, 35; Wilde's debt to, 60
Voltaire, Françoise, 26, 83
Voss, Johann Heinrich, 26

Wainewright, Thomas Griffiths, 44
war, 65
Weeks, Jeffrey, 113 n.5
Weil, Simone, 31; *Gravity and Grace*, 91
Weininger, Otto, *Sex and Character*, 62

32586701

WITHDRAWN
from
STIRLING UNIVERSITY LIBRARY